LOVE LETTERS TO GOD

Love Letters to God

DEVON SPENCER &
KATHERINE WILLIS PERSHEY

foreword by Winn Collier

CASCADE *Books* • Eugene, Oregon

LOVE LETTERS TO GOD

Copyright © 2025 Devon Spencer and Katherine Willis Pershey. All rights reserved. Except for brief quotations in critical publications or reviews, no part of this book may be reproduced in any manner without prior written permission from the publisher. Write: Permissions, Wipf and Stock Publishers, 199 W. 8th Ave., Suite 3, Eugene, OR 97401.

Cascade Books
An Imprint of Wipf and Stock Publishers
199 W. 8th Ave., Suite 3
Eugene, OR 97401

www.wipfandstock.com

PAPERBACK ISBN: 978-1-5326-1890-1
HARDCOVER ISBN: 978-1-4982-4478-7
EBOOK ISBN: 978-1-4982-4477-0

Cataloguing-in-Publication data:

Names: Spencer, Devon, author | Pershey, Katherine Willis, author | Collier, Winn, foreword author.

Title: Love letters to God / Devon Spencer and Katherine Willis Pershey.

Description: Eugene, OR: Cascade Books, 2025 | Includes bibliographical references.

Identifiers: ISBN 978-1-5326-1890-1 (paperback) | ISBN 978-1-4982-4478-7 (hardcover) | ISBN 978-1-4982-4477-0 (ebook)

Subjects: LCSH: Pastoral theology. | Pastoral theology—Biblical teaching. | Interpersonal relations—Religious aspects—Christianity.

Classification: BV4011.3 L75 2025 (paperback) | BV4011.3 (ebook)

VERSION NUMBER 07/25/25

Where noted, Scripture is taken from THE MESSAGE. Copyright © 2002. Used by permission of NavPress Publishing Group.

Where noted, Scripture is taken from the New Revised Standard Version Bible, copyright © 1989, Division of Christian Education of the National Council of the Churches of Christ in the United States of America. Used by permission. All rights reserved.

Where noted, Scripture is taken from THE HOLY BIBLE, NEW INTERNATIONAL VERSION®, NIV® Copyright © 2011 by Biblica, Inc.® Used by permission. All rights reserved worldwide.

Contents

Foreword by Winn Collier | *vii*

Acknowledgments | *ix*

Introduction | *xi*

Interlude: A Text Conversation, September 9, 2022 | 73

Afterword | *177*

Bibliography | *181*

Foreword

YEARS AGO, I GOT into a small spat with a publisher over one of my books, a reworked collection of correspondence from the seventeenth-century French archbishop François Fénelon to friends serving in King Louis's court. I was mesmerized by Fénelon's gentleness, precision, and wisdom—but just as much by the sheer fact that I was reading *letters*. Fénelon, scribbling intimate words to friends amid turmoil and joy and distress, wrote with directness, punchiness, and an unprotected warmth that we rarely find in closely edited works tailored to some faceless audience. Good letters have blood pumping through the sentences.

So, I wanted "letters" in the title. I wanted everyone to know they were invited to peek into someone else's mail. "But, Winn," my publisher said, a little exasperated, "nobody buys books of letters anymore. Nobody reads them."

I held the phone for an awkward moment, stumped and bewildered. "Well, I do," I finally answered. "I read them."

In our isolated and dehumanizing age, I sense the tide may be turning in favor of writing that's more personal and human. And what's more personal than letters? Thankfully, we've experienced renewed interest in Lewis's and Merton's letters (I've especially enjoyed the missives between Merton and Evelyn Waugh). Recently, we've received *The Letters of Emily Dickinson* and *Letters of Note*, that eclectic mix including Gandhi encouraging Hitler to restraint and Queen Elizabeth II sending Dwight Eisenhower her recipe for drop scones.

But again, the best letters are those that pass between genuine friends. When friends converse, the conversation can quickly move past the pleasantries and into the meat. The questions, the disagreements, become clearer. The passion and the hope—and sometimes the wounds—are out in the open. When friends write, we hear what's emerging from the soul.

Foreword

This is why I'm thrilled for this collection of letters between two friends, Katherine and Devon. A pastor and a therapist. One guiding churches for years, one stepping into faith's waters. When I first responded to Katherine after reading these letters, I may have used the *very* literary descriptor: "gobsmacked." The letters were more than I expected. There's so much courage in these pages, such relational and spiritual honesty, such integrity of relationship.

After reading, I leaned back and perused the collection. *This is why we need books of letters*, I said, though there was no one there to hear me.

In our moment, we need people to *show* us the way more than *tell* us the way. We need more stories and examples, less explanation. And that's what you'll find here. These two writers (and goodness, they are both wicked with the pen) wrestle and empathize and tangle and love. There's theological complexity and richness—and not always resolution. There's tension. There's gut-deep laughter. There's forgiveness and tenderness and a dash of snark. It's real life happening on the page.

This is a sinewy work of lived theology, pastoral theology. They show us how to think about God, in community, around difficult themes. They allow us to watch while they *do* friendship, messy and wondrous as it is. They show us how to pastor, how to follow Jesus, how to struggle, how to be a daughter, how to be deluged with grief, how to hold on to hope.

And I want to highlight that word: *hope*. It would be more than easy for this collection, given the places the conversation goes and the people having that conversation, to careen into an infinite pool of cynicism and outrage. But what you will discover instead is a thin, tenacious thread of belligerent hope—an insistence that God is real, which means that despair will never have the final word.

This is good news. This whole collection is good news.

Winn Collier
Director of the Eugene Peterson Center for Christian Imagination at Western Theological Seminary (Holland, MI), Episcopal priest, and author of *Love Big, Be Well: Letters to a Smalltown Church* and *A Burning in My Bones*, the biography of Eugene Peterson

Acknowledgments

Devon

Katherine, who gave me a reason to write and friendship with God between us.

Covenant Presbyterian Church, who gave me a home.

Ian, who taught me about religion.

Alex, who taught me about God. I love you.

Katherine

Devon: the friend I needed then and now.

Winn, Trygve, Mandy, and my Holy Presence friends: a cohort of pastors gathered around God.

The First Congregational Church of Western Springs, which will always be a home even though God has called me to a new community of faith.

First Congregational United Church of Christ in Appleton, where God is doing a new thing.

My favorite people in the whole world: my family. I love you.

Introduction

IN MAY OF 2021, I began a doctor of ministry cohort at Western Theological Seminary. I arrived at the first gathering full of uncertainty; because the entirety of my ministry has unfolded within traditions and congregations with long histories of female pastoral leadership, it was the first time I was to be the only woman in the room in any formal educational or ecclesial setting. During his opening lecture, our lead faculty member, Winn Collier, shared that he hoped we would find "providential friendships" during our studies. I longed for such friendships, and was relieved and grateful that even during that first week I bonded with classmates and began to build meaningful friendships across divisions of denomination, theology, and gender.

When Winn shared those prophetic words about providential friendships, I assumed he meant friendships within the cohort. But in the fall of 2021, a woman named Devon Spencer was referred to the First Congregational Church of Western Springs by a colleague who was familiar with my congregation. She was a very new convert to Christianity and had been reading St. Augustine, Søren Kierkegaard, and Paul Tillich on her own. She attended worship a few times and joined a Bible study I was leading on the book of Job. Sensing our affinity, I invited her to meet me for breakfast. Over oat milk lattes we leapfrogged over anything resembling small talk. Instead we talked about God—God's beauty, mystery, and grace. I'd drained my mug when I announced that I really wanted to know what she thought about Jesus, but first I had to pee. That was good for a giggle, and then, as promised, we continued the conversation at length about the Word Made Flesh. Devon was unsurprisingly drawn to Jesus. She was disinterested in vague spirituality; she craved a robust Christianity.

Toward the end of our time together, I explained that unlike her line of work, which expressly forbids friendships between therapists and their clients, there wasn't quite such a rigid rule for pastors. There is, of course,

Introduction

diversity of opinion and practice on this matter. I can still hear the voice of one of my seminary professors expressly forbidding it. I followed her counsel during my first pastorate, refraining from forming any close friendships with parishioners. When I began my call in Western Springs, I soon learned that one of the primary models for ministry in the context was that of pastor-as-friend. I embraced the model and found it to be not only personally fulfilling, but also a profoundly effective way to minister in the community; it wrested ministry back from the hyper-professionalization of the profession that can result in depersonalized ministry. When *The Christian Century* published a column by M. Craig Barnes offering a searing repudiation of the notion that any pastor could or should ever be friends with a parishioner, I published a set of rebuttals in a rival publication. In retrospect, I think I was protesting too mightily; my bravado veiled insecurity. The fact of the matter is that pastors do need to be mindful of boundaries and not let our own emotional needs crowd out the needs of our people. Still, there's a difference between affirming the importance of boundaries and claiming, as Barnes does, "The pastor offers the congregation's laments and doxology to God and proclaims God's holy word to the congregation. Friendships have little to do with this."[1] These words serve as a sort of anti-prophecy of my friendship with Devon, which has had *everything* to do with this, in a remarkably mutual manner.

It was abundantly clear we were meant to be friends, if there was room on her dance card for a new one. Truly, from that day on our friendship flourished through a flurry of texts, coffee dates, and even one moderately unsuccessful outing to my rock-climbing gym; turns out Devon is not especially keen on heights. By Christmas we were the kind of friends who exchanged gifts. She gave me a copy of her favorite novel, *My Brilliant Friend* by Elena Ferrante, and I gave her a gold cross necklace.

It was not a year into our friendship that I suggested we start exchanging letters. I've always been more deft in writing than speaking, at least when it comes to more complicated theological musings. Some of our text messages were getting a little long. Epistles have long been central to the literature of the church, from Eugene Peterson and Henri Nouwen to St. Paul and St. John, and countless Christians in between. The letters that follow are a spiritual friendship shared in letters. They are both personal and pastoral. They are thoroughly contextual and specific even as they reflect trends in the church. Just as there were quarrels among the Christians in

---

1. Barnes, "Pastor, Not Friend," para 8.

Introduction

Corinth that demanded Paul's apostolic wisdom, there were points of pain in Devon's life that required my compassionate care and vice versa. In an era when even the slightest difference of political or theological opinion can lead to the severing of ties, we offered one another the dignity of commitment; we refused to unfriend a covenantally bound sister in Christ. Through all of this, the project unfurled in real time, encompassing losses we hadn't foreseen and conflicts we probably should have.

In addition to the letters here—which are presented with minimal redaction—we also created an "apocryphal" file in which we exchanged letters that felt too tender to be included in the canon. This proved critical; despite our clarity that the primary letters would have an audience beyond the two of us, there were moments when pastoral and personal confidence was tantamount.

It's daunting to consider these letters being read by others. As the author of two theological memoirs and countless personal essays, I've long known the vulnerability that accompanies publication. But the reason I have formerly taken the risk of writing is the same reason we take this risk now: we believe there is profound value woven into these pages. They reveal two women wrestling with God and sometimes one another, anxious to receive a blessing at dawn. They invite the reader to consider the nature of spiritual friendship and to ponder the enduring problem of suffering. They demonstrate the mustard seed of faith I am tending as a cradle Christian in a mainline Protestant tradition and the fervent faith Devon is cultivating as a new member of a theologically orthodox Presbyterian congregation.

In *Faith Formation in a Secular Age*, Andrew Root names the transformational holiness of ministry; since God ministers to us, we encounter God in and through ministry. "Our lives are bent into the narrative arc of Jesus by allowing Jesus's person to minister to our own person," Root writes. "To help people have faith is to help them experience divine action through the act of being ministered to and ministering to others."[2] These letters show an embodied ministry, a relational ministry, an analog ministry. Through our correspondence and through the providential friendship that continued over tacos and lattes, Devon and I helped one another have faith. Devon and I helped one another encounter God. The trajectory of my life inclines more toward Christ because of this. Thanks be to God.

Katherine Willis Pershey
August 1, 2024

---

2. Root, *Faith Formation in a Secular Age*, 150.

MAY 22, 2022

Dear Katherine,

    I hope you don't come to rue the day you proposed this letter-writing project, because I expect it to be imbalanced; prepare to be inundated. I keep thinking about how Rilke's *Book of Hours* is subtitled *Love Poems to God*, and how ours might be titled *Love Letters to God*. You know how I feel about Rilke—imitation is the most sincere form of flattery—but I also think I'm accurate. I say that knowing that I'm about to wax on about doubt and a whole lot of fear, which would not under normal circumstances make for much of a love letter, but I also think you'll know that love is at the center of even that.

    Love is not something I thought much about prior to my conversion. Love for me was an almost unbearable intensity of emotion, untethered from values or philosophy about what it means to love the right way. It's been so unexpected, learning how to love my neighbor, and also trying. It's not always easy to love the person who's in front of me, and harder still to balance that with care for myself. Pulling it off is incredible, though. I am so relieved I can do it at all, given how chaotically and selfishly I loved before. It's not that I'm always succeeding, but the effort alone has carried me one step closer to peace. I am grateful, but like I mentioned, it weighs on me. Like so much of what's changed for me since converting, it brings both peace and a sword. I hate that I'm fighting the ultimate good, the love that is God, but there's some of that paradox in hearing God speak to me a couple of days ago. There's a heaviness to it I'm not sure I fully understand, but I can't deny its presence.

    I was sitting on my couch, riddled with fear and anxiety over the typical catalyst for those unpleasant emotions, when I heard God tell me, "Don't be afraid." He sounded exasperated, like a parent admonishing his stubborn child for the hundredth time, and I couldn't help but laugh. I imagined him on the verge of pulling his hair out, venting to the angels that he had been sending this message for *months*, and this woman *just won't listen*. It was nice to laugh with God, who is usually so serious for me. As I mentioned over lavender lattes this morning, it was also a tremendous relief. In an instant, everything settled in me. He banished my fear, but mostly it was that he showed up. I haven't been with him much lately, and I hadn't realized just how threatening that distance was starting to feel. It makes me worry that my faith is imperfect, to which I am sure you'll respond that everyone's is, but I'm new to this and doubt feels like a punch in the gut. In any case, the point is that I heard him speak and I believed him.

What surprised me most was how melancholy I felt the next day—Sunday, ironically. I half floated, half dragged through the day, listless and sad and also far less confused than I've been in weeks past. There's a gravity to letting go of fear. A somberness and sobriety that I didn't anticipate. If I accept that in spite of suffering and trauma and loss, I have nothing to fear existentially, spiritually—I'm loved and saved no matter what—it means an end to striving. It means I don't need to rail against circumstance or try to force a reality into being that God hasn't ordained. Why does that salvation also feel like loss? Why shouldn't I want to relinquish to a creator who loves me in a way no human could ever fully emulate, and who sees beyond my wants to give me what I need? At some point in my secular past I heard the phrase "Let go and let God," and it made me want to vomit. I still don't love the cheese factor, but it resonates. Look at the choices I've made independent of Jesus—I need all the help I can get, and I want it. I *want* to trust in God's guidance, but it's too easy to mistake my own ferocious effort for God's will. I think about Ian, and how he shows up whenever I beseech God for answers about the rightness of this person in my life, but is it God bringing us together, or my own stubbornness? Eric, my ex-husband, once described me as "a force," and he didn't intend it as flattery. When I wanted something, I would have it, whatever it took. "No" never meant "no," and in so many ways that got me far. I think now it also blinded me to the many occasions in which I was not meant for something or someone, and they were not meant for me. I still have that in me, but I have suffered for succumbing to this greed, this worship of idols of my own making, and I'm worried I would go so far as to reject God to possess the thing I want. Sometimes, I'm so hell-bent on getting my way that my desires obstruct God from view. Am I doing that now? Insisting on being with someone who upholds our covenant in words but not deeds? When I heard God on my couch, he told me not to be afraid of what is to come in this relationship. I know I shouldn't be, but I stand to lose a lot. I know that if God wants me to have it, I'll get back everything I've given up. If he doesn't, if he wants something else for me, I know it will be exactly what I need. All I can do is wait and trust and not be afraid. Ugh. Ultimately it's easier to put it in God's hands, but right now it feels brutally hard.

I just reread my opening greeting, and I was wrong about filling this letter with doubt. I didn't intend to change directions, but something happened as I wrote that brought me to a surprising place. I probably over-index on assuming divine providence, but I don't really believe in coincidences. I got where I needed to go.

I'm also going to finish that Sue Monk Kidd novel. My faith can't be so fragile that it can't stand up to a fictionalized, fully human Christ. I reacted out of fear, and I've only just received a crystal-clear command not to do that. I told you that I needed a resurrected Christ, and I couldn't stomach Kidd's demystification of the sacred, but I was wrong. I'm not afraid of her secular Christ, because in my heart of hearts I know there's no such thing. I want to read a moving, faithful, literary depiction of the resurrection, but I won't fall apart if she can't give me that. I will not disparage her beliefs, but what I believe is that she's wrong. I take great comfort in that.

After God told me not to be afraid, he called me "Daughter." How could I possibly turn away from that?

With love,
Devon

MAY 9, 2022

Dear Devon,

I'm hereby establishing that I will not begin every letter to you with an apology—sorry I didn't respond sooner, etc.—because you've made it clear that you understand my life. The fullness of vocation, family, doctoral studies, etc. I drench myself in a Sabbath spirit on Mondays, and then the rest of the week is a marathon. Anyway: today is Monday, and we don't have plans for breakfast today, so instead I'm taking a few moments to respond.

I also won't start every letter with a litany of how much I adore you, but since this is the first I'm playing that card unapologetically. Paul started lots of his letters with swoony thanksgivings for the people on the other end of the epistle—"I thank my God every time I remember you," etc. And I do. Thank God. These can indeed be love letters to God because sometimes it seems to me that your sheer existence, your sudden presence in my life, is a love letter from God. It's hard for me to express how badly I needed our friendship. Not just someone like you. Precisely you, with your astonishing intellect, your relational trauma, your faith that seems, paradoxically, delicate as a dandelion and fierce as a lion. It seems like faith is a gift that was foisted on you and you weren't sure it fit you but you were too stubborn to return it, even after the giver of the gift proved yet another source of pain. But I think you know, the gift wasn't from Ian. God has a sense of humor—dare I call it a wicked sense of humor—and Ian was just the right mediator to bring the gospel of Jesus Christ to the Force that is Devon Spencer. I want to reclaim that language, even if it wasn't meant kindly before. I experience you as a force, too, but a force of life, a force of honesty, a force of healing, a force of renewal.

My sense is that your faith is not softening your intellect or dulling your force. My sense is that your faith—your ongoing attunement to the Triune God—is giving you access to wisdom. True wisdom. Though I generally hate the word "godly"—who dares make God an adjective?!—I'm tempted to reclaim that word too. I think you are encountering godly wisdom, and you assent to it because . . . well, why would you not? You know what poison tastes like. And this is not poison. It is goodness, freedom, resurrection. It is fearlessness, reverence, and salvation. It is the God who is God calling you Daughter. How could you possibly turn away from that, indeed?

I have two choices now—hold onto this and finish it later, or send it along now, in this woefully incomplete state. I have more to say, but I have a preschool luncheon to attend. Yes, on my day off—every so often I make exceptions. I know you are full of letters, and that this is just the beginning, so I will sign off with great anticipation for the next round.

With love and grace and peace,
Katherine

May 9, 2022

Dear Katherine,

 I write this with a glass of wine in one hand and a Xanax making its way into my bloodstream. My day differed from yours, but it has been a DAY nonetheless. I'm thinking about you right now, though. You and your pained and panicked children (through no fault of your own), and how this must weigh on your heart. It can be such a burden to care as much as you do, and I imagine how your concern for others might sometimes feel as powerful as possession, and though you have no choice but worry, help, solve, and worry again.

 You could only feel that much anxiety with as much love as you have—talk about a force. It might be the best thing about you, how deeply and thoroughly you love. I feel enveloped by it, but never suffocated. I mentioned in my last letter that I'm learning how to love the right way, and I think God brought us together in large part because you're a living, breathing example of someone who strives to do just that. It feels contagious. I'm not sure if you always pull it off, being as human as the next person, but damn it do you try. Your preternaturally high tolerance for dysfunction doesn't hurt either, because I, like you, am a *lot*. Thank God Jesus loves sinners. I'm not clean now, but neither am I such a danger to myself and others anymore. The hope I have now undercuts the desperation that ruled me, so I can afford to be less desperate. It feels like only five minutes ago that I was, though, and I worshiped that brokenness in me. When I was "dating" (numbing my pain with men) one of my favorite first date questions was "What's the worst thing you've ever done?" What kind of monster asks that on a first date?? I lived to titillate. When they asked me the same question, I almost always lied. I would cop to enough that it was believable, but I could never detail the worst of the worst. I don't know if it would feel shameful telling you, or like expiation. You like that, expiation? I busted out that Catholic morsel just for you, since I know you live for a little papist flair.

 But anyway, do you think such a thing exists as too much sin? Too much darkness? Maybe we're all forgiven, but what's all this business about judgment day? Forgiveness seems like smoke and mirrors in the context of judgment to follow. What does it matter if we're forgiven, if we're then condemned for . . . I don't even know what would be the tipping point in wickedness. Perhaps I am too new to the faith to know how to reconcile those two major tenets of Christianity, but I suspect a bevy of seasoned Christians stumble over the same hurdle, because no one has yet been able to make sense of it for me. Judgment in a court of law is punishment for a crime, and how am I to believe that I am forgiven if God convicts me out of the other side of his mouth? I love the mysteries of Scripture, but I can feel the anxieties around them mounting, and I don't know for how much longer I can accept them at face value.

On the train home from *Madame Butterfly*, before the pandemic, I told Ian, in a "don't get your hopes up" kind of way, that I was starting to feel drawn to the God of our faith. I hadn't read so much as a page of Scripture, but I had recently cracked open the pages of Augustine's *Confessions*, my first theology, and it moved me. Despite my protestations, he predicted I would not only claim the Christian God as my own, but would develop an unquenchable thirst for inquiry, reflection, and debate. He described intellectual Christians who gravitate towards one another for inquiry, reflection, and debate, and whose cerebral thoughts and complicated feelings revolved not around themselves, but God. I called bullshit at the time, but I can feel myself turning into exactly that. Curiosity and questioning are integral to who I am, but it's a whole different ball game when the answer to every conceivable question is "faith." It seems like circular logic, but I'm nearing a point where I need to move beyond that kind of elliptical understanding. When it comes down to it, it's all just a story we choose to believe in, but I hate that. Even as I typed that I felt my heart ache in my chest, like it knows something my intellect does not. Perhaps as a pastor, but also a person who I know has questioned, you can offer some guidance.

With more gratitude than I can bear,
Devon

May 14, 2022

Dear Devon,

First, I want to tell you about my father-in-law while he still breathes. I like him. I've always liked him, so much that it felt a little awkward to be so drawn to his loud laugh and boyish enthusiasm when Benjamin's relationship with his father had sometimes been a source of pain. Before Parkinson's disease took Ed's mind, it was sharp. He has a PhD in history, with a focus on industrial history, but he wasn't a stodgy academic. For years he worked at the Western Reserve Historical Society museum, where he was eager to point out the salient details of fancy cars and the Euclid Beach Park carousel, which had been restored and installed in the museum. He's the one who taught me what constitutes a true carousel. If the animals rising and falling to the band organ are zebras and monkeys, it is a mere merry-go-round. Carousels only have horses. This is the kind of thing you can learn from the internet, but it's better to learn it from a father-in-law with bright white hair, an inability to suffer fools, and a penchant for root beer floats. The last time I had a root beer float was years ago, with Ed. We decided we would have root beer floats every time we got together. But then years passed and we didn't see them. At first we were hurt. Benjamin didn't exactly say he'd told me so, but he did acknowledge, yes, this sudden and inexplicable lack of interest in my life is not new. He'd felt that hurt before. But then it became clear that Ed wasn't well. They hunkered down. Pandemic, etc. The next time I saw him his swallowing reflex was still functioning. We should have had our root beer floats, but it felt like such a silly thing to bring up, so I didn't. And now his swallowing reflex has deteriorated. He can take some water with a sponge. Years ago he asked me if I'd do his funeral, even though he doesn't really believe in God. I said no. I told him I needed to be a daughter-in-law on that day. I regret that decision more than I can say. And now, I might not even be there, if he dies when I am in Montana.

You ask about judgment. Judgment doesn't frighten me because I am so thoroughly convinced of God's grace. Yes, there is biblical evidence to the contrary. Sheep and goats, etcetera. I believe God's love is too immense not to redeem all of creation. I believe in a holy refining fire; I welcome it. *Take away the stain of sin and shame and make me new, O Laundress of Heaven.* It won't hurt more than the sin and shame did. I broke up with a boyfriend once because he told me he believed Buddhists were going to hell. Bullshit. It's not that it doesn't matter whether or not we believe in God—I believe God is God whether we praise him or not—but I don't think God gives up on a single soul he crafted in his endless creativity.

It's all a story we choose to believe in. Faith is never certainty. But it's such a good and beautiful story; such a good and beautiful faith. I believe it's true. I don't think there's anything wrong with being an intellectual Christian that debates, ponders, challenges, and analyzes. I like that kind of Christian. The only problem is to be a Christian who doesn't love. That's an oxymoron for you: unloving Christian. We get this wrong so much, of course—it's why the public perception of Christians is so poor. It's such a tragedy, given that we purportedly follow Jesus, who is "the reflection of God's glory and the exact imprint of God's very being," to quote the quirky Letter to the Hebrews. And over and over and over again, that reflection and imprint is revealed to be love. Not theoretical love. Love in-the-flesh. Sacrificial love. Compassionate love. Generous love. You defined it perfectly when you spoke to Moms in Faith last week. I think this is why we need one another—you and I specifically, and Christians generally. We cannot love God without loving neighbor. We cannot follow Christ without breaking bread. We cannot be saved without surrendering our darkness to God's perfect light.

Maybe that last one made you catch your breath. You think you're too dark for grace, too recently a "monster" to escape righteous wrath. I hate to break it to you, but that's just not how it works. You know that Jesus was always getting in trouble for hanging out with so-called monsters, right? And when they called him on it, he said, "I have not come to call the righteous but sinners to repentance." The darkness can never overcome the light. You are free.

And now, to Montana.

Love,
Katherine

May 15, 2022

Dear Katherine,

   I'm so sorry about Ed. Whenever you mention him, I see Benjamin's face reading that brief, heartbreaking passage at Words and Music. His voice haunts me. He sounded so calm. I felt in a way like a voyeur into his soul, because of what you've shared with me about his relationship with his dad. Like I shouldn't be intruding, but I had to. I felt all the pain of my own damaged parental relationships, the resentment and anger that burned so hot for so long, and the guilt that would follow. I felt the strength and stoicism in his choice to nourish his dying father, even as his own wounds gaped open. I think of Benjamin now as his father approaches death—for real, this time—and I think of you in Montana, on that imperfectly timed trip. I hope to God you don't torture yourself if Ed dies while you're gone, because you had Benjamin's blessing to go, and because I don't think you are needed in the sense we sometimes are in times of death. I think of the unfulfilled promise of root beer floats and the unshared knowledge of a PhD holder who failed his son, but who you get a kick out of. Maybe you even love him. But I keep going back to Benjamin. I imagine him getting the call, strong and stoic as he was at that reading, but inside weathering the hurricane of emotions that is complicated grief. I've spoken to Benjamin about twice, but I really like him, Katherine. I like him and I want so badly for him to be okay. Is it too late for you to do his funeral? I should say now that if I die before you, I want you to do mine.

   I tried to explain Christian love to my mother today, and I'm not confident it landed. We're consumed by individualism in this country, and it feels increasingly impossible to sell someone on self-sacrifice. I wanted her to see the beauty of a panoramic love that protects not only the well-being of the self, but also the other, even occasionally (gasp) at the self's expense. Imagine a world in which inconveniencing ourselves was no hardship, but a gift to another in need, and a social landscape steadied by the assurance that we will get back what we give. In this world, especially in individualistic areas, we are misers with our love, as though to give is to lose, and we err in that thinking. I cannot conceive of anything more beautiful than a neverending cycle of grace, but my explanations evoke defensiveness born out of fear, and I understand why. We've all been hurt at the hands of someone we love, and some of us never forget it. We lose ourselves in the vigilance of trying to prevent it from ever reoccurring, and protect ourselves out of the good relationships that might be waiting down the road. Hurt people don't always know how to give without suffering.

My mother also asked me about confession. Her parents raised her Catholic, and she hated it. It doesn't sound like she had much spiritual direction, and the only lesson she seems to have learned was that she should feel guilty about . . . everything. Confession doesn't make sense to her, so I tried to explain why I find that accountability essential, and why we should do penance. I'm not exactly sure what I mean by "penance," but I think we're responsible for replenishing the good we drained from the world with our sins. We should do it to ease the sickness in our souls. God unconditionally loves every wretched hair on our heads, but we can't extend the same grace to ourselves. Or at least I can't, not always. I am trying, but for me to inch closer to love, I need to first pass through shame. I don't understand this moment we're in, pretending like shame can't be useful. It helps me to feel bad for being bad, because it helps me want to be good. Please don't be like everyone else, and tell me I'm not bad. It's my legacy as a human, and I have an exceptional talent for it when pressed. The difference is that when I'm bad now, I try harder to be good. I will inconvenience myself so that someone I've hurt feels newly loved, and as basic as that gesture sounds, it was never second nature to me. I am learning forgiveness, a punishing process, and offering it again and again to someone who can't help but hurt me over and over, because I know his heart and I pity his limitations and it's not love to demand of him what he can't, in every sense of that word, give. Am I describing penance, or love? Are they different?

I don't know if this is in the spirit of confession or anxiety, but I am afraid for you on this trip. I am projecting my own fears all over you, and I am afraid you will feel how I would feel if I could not be present at a time of grief. My anxiety makes me want to write yet again that *I don't think you should have stayed (!!!!!!!!)*, and frets that your self-forgiveness won't come readily. It wrings its hands over the possibility you will beat yourself up for being there, because you wouldn't deserve that battering. I worry over this in the spirit of love—I don't want you to suffer. Not ever, but especially not more than is your lot. I want you to live a life of stability, replete with healthy emotional boundaries, a balance of self and other, and objectivity about what constitutes shameful acts. I want so, so much more for you than what I have with myself (I am working on it, I swear), and I would do everything in my power to help you have it. So, yeah, maybe this is just love.

I love you, Katherine. Be well out there.
Devon

May 17, 2022

Dear Katherine,

I can't tell you how wrong it feels to write to you about my musings on death while you're in the throes of experiencing one. That beast, Selfishness, rears its ugly head again, and I'm sorry. This could easily be a letter for another time—I'm not making a sensitive choice—and still I cannot stop myself from writing it. In a yearlong discourse about God and humanity and love, one can reasonably expect that death will come up again, but it's hounding me *right now*. It's so selfish. I'm sorry. Another part of me knows that you, specifically you, would welcome theological reflection about what you're going through; it's your lens, and I would bet money that you're already in process, out there in Montana. I hope you're doing it amidst those towering trees or sitting next to that glassy lake in the photos you've sent. I hope your cohort is helping you in some way. If I'm wrong, if academic grief is not what you need, put this letter down. It will be enough for me to have written it.

So much trauma has swirled around me lately. Everyone seems to be dying or breaking up or getting sick. On multiple occasions someone has said to me or I to them, "This is too much—you need a break," as though that's how this all works. It *is* too much and we *do* need a break, but the fact is that we might not get one. If we might not get one, I don't know how wise it is to hold out hope for one. To chant "tomorrow, tomorrow, tomorrow" to ourselves, as though suffering has a beginning and an end. None of our suffering is acute, though. It is a constant, a backdrop of our lives on earth, and expecting tomorrow to bring an end to it is naive.

Built into the Somatic Experiencing (SE) model is the concept of rest. Without it, our nervous systems will glitch out completely and God only knows what happens thereafter. Actually, I do know. It means moving through a world in a continuous state of stress and agitation that affects you down to your organs. Literally. I've been there and it broke me, probably more than once, but I was so disconnected from myself that I wouldn't have made the connection. Anyway, we need rest. In SE, though, we know that rest doesn't usually mean vacation. I mean it's great if you can get one, but we aim for accessibility in our interventions. We build in rest in small moments: in the lull between spikes in our sympathetic nervous system; the ninety seconds of appreciation of the pillow holding up our heads; or the calm, like snow settling, that envelops us when we stroke the dog that stands between us and abject loneliness. We know better than to imagine we can rewire the nervous system with a vacation. We do it incrementally, over time, in small doses.

I think this is how we have to approach the existential suffering that is life. I wonder how the world would look without The Fall, or the entire Old Testament for that matter. What if early on, humans so appreciated God's love that we wouldn't have dreamed of turning away from it? Would that mean a world not sinking into sin, and would that then mean that suffering wouldn't be so banal, like it is in our world? It's easy to read Scripture literally, and decide that we suffer because Adam and Eve made a foolish choice in the garden—essentially, that we brought unnecessary suffering upon ourselves. That linear equation doesn't *not* make sense, but I wonder if it's complete.

The therapist in me thinks not. Is that wrong, to challenge divinely inspired wisdom with psychology? Add it to the list of blasphemies, I guess. The therapist in me, or more likely, the woman in me who has witnessed so much ugliness she cannot in good conscience look away, suspects that God always knew we would let him down. All-knowing, all-seeing God, who sees into our hearts and knows us better than ourselves, couldn't possibly have been surprised when his project went awry. Right? Doesn't it seem strange to imagine that he was shocked that Adam and Eve ate the apple? Like he hadn't himself given us the wide eyes and wandering hearts of curious children? We could not have surprised him with our error in the garden.

Let's say that God knew exactly what he was creating. He never intended to make gods out of humans, so it follows he knew that we would live ungodly lives. God does not lack reason, and to suggest otherwise is to question his omniscience. But if he anticipated our fallibility, isn't that kind of a dick move? What kind of benevolent grand plan is it to birth an entire species who were doomed to hurt each other and themselves? To sin like their lives depended on pleasure, not salvation? Isn't that a little psychopathic, when it comes down to it? I'm having a little bit of a "fuck you, God" moment, but I imagine he gets it.

Then again, and this is surely blasphemy, maybe his omnipotence has limitations, and maybe he knew that. What if God knew that while he was divine, whole, and capable of giving orders to the morning, that he could not create creatures entirely in his image? Not that parents possess any of those qualities, but there's a parallel to be drawn between a God who knew his flock would fail him, and parents who accept that their kids, however beloved and special, will be riddled with flaws. We don't have kids so that they'll be perfect; we have them because we love the idea of having them. We love the idea of loving our children, who in turn love us back, even when they hate us. The love and custodianship is the point of having children, and that might have been God's motivation as well. He knew that he would spend eons watching us suffer, grieving and intervening and soaking up secondary trauma that no therapist would ever be able to unburden. He took up his own cross in creating us in the first place, and that's the kind of God I want to believe in.

I think the way God alleviates suffering is like an SE practitioner: sometimes he gives us breaks. Sometimes, when we can't handle it anymore, he opens our eyes to a fleeting glimpse of the divine. He wakes us from a prophetic nightmare, blesses us with a friend who will stand with us through our suffering, or leads us to a shelter dog who will go on to provide the kind of unconditional love we lacked in the marriage that just ended. He won't keep us from sinning, warfare, pestilence, or death itself, but sometimes he pries open our hearts so that we can receive the love that has always enveloped us.

He cannot and will not make us into Gods, but he will make us immortal.

I love you so much right now,
Devon

MAY 18, 2022

Dear Devon,

 When I saw that you sent a second letter yesterday, before I even had a chance to respond to the last, I felt so loved. Such a gift, knowing you had sat down, held me in your heart, and written not one but two more love letters to God—even if you did get a little feisty with God in the second one. I am kicking myself for failing to pack my laptop for this trip to Flathead Lake. I imagined myself reading, hiking, and fellowshipping with friends during down times. I didn't want to get drawn into work, and I didn't expect to have energy for writing. But it turns out this week is structured so generously and the sun lingers in the sky so lazily there is plenty of time for everything.

. . .

 Those are the words I started Montana, typing awkwardly on a glitchy secondhand tablet before giving up and taking a nap. Now I am back in Illinois, having traveled to Ohio and back to catch the tail end of the events meant to honor Ed. I watched the recording of the funeral, and it tore me up to see my beloved Benjamin struggle to read words of sacred Scripture, his voice thick with tears. He told me later that when he heard himself begin to cry, he heard his own father's voice breaking with emotion. Ed had a boisterous laugh, as the obituary recalled, but he also had something even more precious: the capacity to cry. I pity people who can't do it. I told you before that Benjamin spent most of his childhood living hundreds of miles away from his dad. After the divorce and Ed's remarriage, he and Monica moved to New Jersey, and later to Massachusetts. They weren't back in Ohio until Benjamin was in college. So Benjamin and Jennifer would spend a few weeks out east with their dad, plus holidays. And at the end of these times, they'd have to say goodbye. It was never not painful. And Ed wasn't afraid to show his sorrow. He'd tear up as he hugged his kids goodbye, Benjamin's bright red bowl cut coming away from those embraces a little wet from the tears falling on his head. I experienced a few of these partings myself over the years; once, after a particularly joyous Christmastide visit when we were new parents, Ed was overcome with grief when it was time to head back to LAX.

 I first witnessed Ed's emotive grief when he spoke at his own father's committal at the Slovenian cemetery in Joliet, just weeks after Benjamin and I married. I do not remember what he said to honor his father, but I remember how he sounded when he said it. And it was precisely how Benjamin sounded when he tried to form the words of the psalmist last Friday. It was no wonder the tenor of his own voice left him trembling: it was as if Ed himself was speaking. I wondered aloud to Benjamin if, perhaps, one of the reasons Ed Junior wept at his father's committal was because he heard Ed Senior when he opened his mouth to speak. How many generations does it go back, these sons weeping for their imperfect, beloved fathers?

It killed me not to be there to hug him when he returned to his seat in the front row of the funeral home. But Genevieve was there to console him, to lean her little head onto his shoulder and soak up some of his tears with her ponytail.

Devon, this is my grief talking, but it is also my slant response to your pondering about God and God's questionable wisdom in creating humankind, with our capacity for depravity. God is love. So much so that it isn't sufficient for God to be a lonely deity playing solitaire in an empty universe. God is love so radically that God is inherently in relationship, even within God's own self. You know this, but I love to repeat the names, especially since I am only just allowing myself the thrill of reclaiming the old language: Father, Son, and Holy Spirit. In seminary we were taught to avoid the classic Triune formula for the persons of the Trinity, because it is unfeminist to call God Father. But Creator, Redeemer, and Sustainer don't quite have the same effect. They aren't related to one another. They are job descriptions. Epic ones, but job descriptions nonetheless.

I believe you are absolutely right: this Triune God of love loved the idea of having us, of making us in his image and delighting at our sheer existence. But relationships are only real when both parties are free. God can command us to love God with all our hearts and minds and strength, and to love our neighbors as ourselves. But God cannot make us do it.

I don't so much think of Adam and Eve as the ancestral culprits, the schmucks who screwed it all up for everyone. Adam and Eve, to my mind, are archetypes upon which we hang our bewilderment at the world. We have this sneaking suspicion that there is something good and holy at the genesis of all that is seen and unseen, and we have an equally profound dismay at the state of things. *Something must have happened.* Have you ever noticed that the biblical narrative begins in a garden and ends in a city? I love this detail, which I did not see until someone pointed it out to me. The humans are placed in paradise and given everything—food, freedom, intimacy with one another and with God. And they disobey, breaking their relationship with the One in whose image they were so lovingly crafted. God spends an enormous amount of time and energy—and blood and sweat—on the work of reconciliation, restoration, repair, redemption, resurrection. But in the end, it is not a matter of return. We do not go back to the garden. Instead, the book of Revelation imagines the reunion of God and God's people in the city of Jerusalem:

> See, the home of God is among mortals.
> He will dwell with them;
> they will be his peoples,
> and God himself will be with them and be their God,
> he will wipe every tear from their eyes.
> Death will be no more;
> mourning and crying and pain will be no more,
> For the first things have passed away. (Rev 21:3–4 NRSV)

Jerusalem is a real place, but I tend to think this does not mean that God will be limited to a singular postal code. Naming the Holy City gives us permission to name our own neighborhoods. The home of God is Flathead Lake, and Cleveland Heights, and Bucktown, and Western Springs. And even in these places, God will wipe every tear from our eyes, and death will be no more. This is the kind of God I want to believe in, too.

Your fury at the suffering and trauma, though—I feel this in my bones. What difference does it make that someday, in the fullness of time, there will be healing, if people are still brutalizing one another in the here and now? I keep telling you I want to reread *The Brothers Karamazov*, and one of the reasons I want to do so is to find out if I still react to it the same way I did when I read it at nineteen. I rejected Alyosha's faith. I scoffed at his hope. I want to read it again as a sort of literary thermometer—can I tolerate his appeal to eschatology in the face of injustice, perhaps even embrace it?

In the meantime: I am praying for you, and for all the people you love who are suffering. Benjamin also read the Beatitudes for his father's service, so imagine my good husband speaking those words for you, too: *blessed are those who mourn, for they shall be comforted.*

I want to tell you more about Montana, and my intentions to spend the foreseeable future interiorizing and praying Psalm 1. I want to meditate more on the providential "breaks" I received from our divine Somatic Experiencing Practitioner. Soon.

Love,
Katherine

P.S. Isn't that text from Revelation just exquisite?

May 23, 2022

Dear Katherine,

    I tried to respond to your beautiful, soulful letter last night, but I was so battered from that training that my body kicked me right out of itself. Itself? Is that the right reflexive pronoun? Do I even need a reflexive pronoun here? Whatever. Learning how to treat trauma means re-experiencing so much of my own that it feels like running a gauntlet. We practice on each other, and while they pretend to protect us with the imperative to pick a "mild" trauma memory when we act as the "client," they do so with the knowledge that our systems do not compartmentalize so neatly. I couldn't tolerate the implicit memories electrocuting my system, and when I sat down to respond I realized I couldn't feel anything, so I couldn't write anything. The words were stilted and too carefully chosen, and I didn't recognize myself. Your letter deserved better than that, so here I am, less distressed but possibly a little mad from the reverberations, trying to do it justice now.

    God bless Ed. God bless Ed and Benjamin and you and Genevieve and her ponytail. I'm so sorry for your loss and for the distance from his death you endured. I expect most sons weep for their imperfect, beloved fathers. Not that daughters don't, but because men's relationships are often so emotionally impoverished, I imagine they could drown in an ocean of unresolved feelings. That's a generalization but I stand by it. These sons grow up with role models who keep their loved ones at arm's length from their hearts. There's so much fear in men about love, especially love with other men (friends, children) and it breaks my heart. I think it breaks their son's hearts too, and it shows up in dysfunction, anger, and regret. I know little about my paternal grandfather, but I'm told he worked a great deal. My father didn't say this, but I get the sense that he looked up at his own father on the pedestal he placed him on, and from that vantage point the affair with his career must have seemed small in comparison to his towering presence. I never met my grandfather, but it sounds like his work took him away from his family, and my grandmother kept it all together. My formidable Quaker grandmother, with her master's degree and her late-in-life children. I worry that my father will never forgive himself for not being enough and giving enough to his father, but I suspect he has little to forgive himself for. He was in his twenties when his father died of brain cancer, not old enough to appreciate his parents, and not wise enough to notice the trauma their imperfections incurred. So, God bless my dad as well.

You know what's wild? That the father/son relationship between God and Jesus was perfection, and here we are trying to teach mortal men to feel. I pray this is one of the first things that will pass away.

I didn't know that the biblical narrative ends in a city, nor had I heard that passage from Revelation. I feel so young admitting that. I feel young all the time on this spiritual journey. I care so much and I feel so much, but I know so little. Ian tried to assure me it didn't matter, and that many of the early Christians would never have read Scripture, but I still say it does matter. How can I call myself a Christian if I don't know the story? The full story. I'm in Kings and 2 Chronicles right now, and the more I advance the more it becomes irrefutably clear that the full story matters. One detail can change the meaning of a message, and as it is I miss many details.

But yes, that text *is* exquisite. "For the first things have passed away" (Rev 21:4); what a relief. What a good thing to have died. That's the sense I get—that it's a death of sorts. The passing of a brutal era. Of ire and sin and uncertainty and destruction and faithlessness. I hear the imagery in Revelation terrifies, but I'm guessing it's the terror of that refining fire. Maybe we all have to walk through fire to get to God. I did.

If I were writing an essay I would be agonizing over the narrative flow, fretting that this next paragraph has a natural connection to my reflection on fathers and *how can I just plunk it down here*? Thankfully it's a letter and I can plunk it down wherever I please. Or wherever it ends up because of a wandering mind and poor planning, but it is what it is, and what it is is right here:

Why do we need "Creator, Redeemer, and Sustainer"? You know I am a feminist, but that means equality for all; it doesn't mean we neuter all gendered terminology. I understand the argument that God personified as male upholds a patriarchal power structure—that it sanctifies it. I get it, but personally, I don't care. It's a pronoun; it's not God. Jesus was male, and I really hope we're not about to try and refute that on the grounds of feminism. He simply was. He was male, and I'm fine with that. He called God "Father," and I'm fine with that. When I am with God, and when I've heard him speak to me, it's a male presence I feel. What's more, I mourn the tradition of the ages that disintegrates when we rework foundational terminology. Genesis makes it plain: men *and* women were made in God's image, and if women are also reflections then God is genderless. I care little whether we consider him male or female, but for me, personally for me, I will call him Father.

This illustrates nothing about women. We are no less holy, no less beloved, and certainly no less capable than men of communing with God and the Christian community (see above for speculative evidence that we, at home in Relationship and with our variable, tortuous feelings, are far more equipped to lead a congregation into relationship with God). One of my all-time-favorite New Testament moments is when one of Jesus's disciples expresses incredulity that Jesus is conversing thoughtfully with a woman, and Jesus basically tells him to fuck off. One day I'll have enough of a grasp on Scripture to provide a direct reference, but I know it's in John, and John is a poet.

And speaking of poets, my frenzied mind has to insert another thoughtlessly placed paragraph.

I'm over halfway through *My Bright Abyss,* and the truth and beauty are almost more than I can bear. At one point, Wiman unknowingly comes to the defense of the part of me abashed at the paradox of my fervor and the newness of my spirituality. Sometimes I feel embarrassed when I catch myself in passionate discourse, like I don't have a right to speak so boldly about something I know so little about. In these moments I feel like a child in a room full of adults, unaware of how small I am until all of a sudden it's all I can think about, but Wiman says, "Intellectuals and artists concerned with faith tend to underestimate the radical, inviolable innocence it requires.... Innocence, for the believer, remains the only condition in which intellectual truths can occur."[1] This might be another letter entirely, but for now I want to state for the record, emphatically, that I believe this to be true.

To innocence,
Devon

---

1. Wiman, *My Bright Abyss,* 63–64.

May 28, 2022

Dear Devon,

 Ah: *My Bright Abyss*. Never have I spent so much ink on a book. I underlined dozens of sentences and starred hundreds of passages. More pages are marked than not. It almost hurt to read that book, it was so excruciatingly beautiful. "Sorrow is so woven through us," Wiman writes, "so much a part of our souls, or at least any understanding of our souls that we are able to attain, that every experience is dyed with its color. This is why, even in moments of joy, part of that joy is the seams of ore that are our sorrow. They burn darkly and beautifully in the midst of joy, and they make joy the complete experience that it is. But they still burn."[1] As much as I loved his ruminations about the nature of belief and doubt, and, *my God*, that line he assigns to Christ about getting off your "mystified ass" and doing something,[2] this bit about joy and sorrow was and is staggering to me. I had a gasp of recognition, having this long-standing inability to experience uncomplicated joy. I think I learned from *My Bright Abyss* that there is no such thing as uncomplicated joy. Maybe happiness can be simple but joy is inherently complicated, because life is inherently complicated. And, indeed, sorrowful.

 The seams were burning brightly during my time in Montana. The sorrow of Benjamin's grief and my absence, the sorrow of the shooting in Buffalo. And even though it happened days after my return, the sorrow of Uvalde is coloring my rapidly fading memories. How can we live in a world that contains such extremes? But we do. And I don't want to relinquish the joy. So here's my testimony of joy. Flathead Lake is exquisite; the kind of lake that has a full complement of moods. It never looked the same twice. One morning it would be calm and blue-green; by that afternoon it would be a tempestuous silver, thwarting my kayaking aspirations. My cabin at the Flathead Lutheran Bible Camp was surprisingly comfortable compared to the rustic dump I'd conjured in my imagination. The kitchen was stocked with a seemingly endless supply of loose leaf teas, including my longtime favorite Evening in Missoula. Our schedule was minimal—worship and class every morning, and a wide expanse of time for whatever else we needed the rest of the time.

1. Wiman, *My Bright Abyss*, 19.
2. Wiman, *My Bright Abyss*, 84.

I loved morning worship each day. The simplicity of sitting in a circle with a songbook, a couple of guitars, and a cajon—I just loved it. It's not that I don't appreciate the formality of worship in the United Church of Christ— I do. Pipe organs echo the music of the spheres, as far as I'm concerned, and I'll love them until I die and fully expect all the stops to be pulled for my funeral processional. But oh, I do love an acoustic guitar strumming along to a folk hymn. I recorded a few songs on my cell phone, wanting to capture the hearty sound of more than twenty uninhibited pastors praising God. Our voices filled the space so completely I could imagine our voices filling the whole valley, the music bouncing off the surface of the water and reaching all the way to the far mountains. I could have sung for hours, but after two songs we would turn to Scripture and prayer. What we did was lovely, but I missed the prayers we've used to begin our time together in the previous doctoral intensives, adapted from the Northumbria community. I've been mildly obsessed with the *Celtic Daily Prayer* book I purchased after our first gathering in May 2021. The Morning Prayer liturgy includes a line from John's Gospel, words Peter utters: "To whom shall we go? You have the words of eternal life" (John 6:68). I love that plaintive question, how it braids together rhetoric, reverence, and exasperation. Once you've realized that Christ speaks the words of life—that Christ *is* the Word of life—where the hell else are we supposed to go? But, again, we didn't pray these words, and it took me a minute to let go of my grief. I'm a sucker for ritual, for tradition. *Familiar* and *family* quite obviously share an etymology. A familiar prayer might as well be my sister; a familiar litany, my brother.

Speaking of my brothers. Have I mentioned how much I love my cohort? I felt such apprehension about being the only female participant in this doctor of ministry program, and the only pastor affiliated with a liberal tradition. It's true, there are some conversations I avoid having with them because I suspect our convictions would be at odds. I just don't have the heart to contemplate that these men I love and respect don't believe you-know-who should be in love with her transmasculine partner. Perhaps this is a betrayal of my queer beloveds. I nonetheless set those matters aside and enter into the fellowship of this cohort, embracing all that we do share. Etymology, again: "cohort" comes from the French word meaning "company of soldiers, band of warriors."[3] We may be a company, we may be a band, but there is nothing militaristic about our contingency. One of the members joked that we are a "company of frauds"—an acknowledgment that none

---

3. See https://www.etymonline.com/search?q=cohort.

of us ever knows what we're doing. You're lucky if you have a pastor who is aware of his or her own insufficiency. I think that's what we share in common, as much as our love for Eugene Peterson: we know the depth of our need for God's grace.

I may have missed our traditional morning prayer but I did not miss the sterile classroom in Holland. In Montana we had class by a roaring fire. By that fire, Winn dared us to stand in the middle of a crumbling world and proclaim that Jesus is Lord, and to look for all the places Christ is playing (there are, according to the poet Gerard Manley Hopkins, ten thousand). Eugene's son Eric talked about how the sacraments "condition our senses to perceive the sacred everywhere." He also invited us to consider ourselves Eugene's legacy, and claimed that the only way we can do this is to be ourselves, to minister as ourselves—no one else.

This whole business about "being yourself" has been such a long, slow, and profound unfolding in my life. I've both loved and hated that phrase, depending on what it means. "Do what you want, regardless of the needs of others" is so toxic. The cult of individualism. But when "being yourself" is about fully embracing the person God has created you to be: yes. Yes! I love these words from *Love's Long Line* by Sophfronia Scott:

> There is a virtue of a name so unique that you can embody it, become it. It's like I had a headstart in defining myself before anyone else could do it for me. This early foundation, I think, contributed to my positive outlook—my name gives me confidence and that confidence makes it easier for me to believe the world is for and not against me. I have built on this foundation, refining the question of who I want to be for myself and others to the point where I have developed this mission: to become so much my name, to fill it with pure soul, that it becomes adjective and more. *I am Sophfronia—That is very Sophfronia—How Sophfronia.* And people who know me know, without question, what that adjective means.[4]

That passage just cracked me open. It made me long to become more Katherine, to fill my ordinary name with so much pure soul that the people who know me know, without question, what that adjective means. I know you are sorting out what it means to be "so very Devon," and I can tell you I delight in your Devonness.

I digress: back to the classes by the fire. Mandy really mixed things up by having us dance. Really. And yes, though I only just met the sole female

---

4. Scott, *Love's Long Line*, 88.

faculty since she's from Australia, I can affirm that encouraging a bunch of middle-aged pastors to prance around to an expertly curated playlist is *very* Mandy. I might not have been able to let go and get down if the second song hadn't been a favorite from Over the Rhine. Finally, on the last morning, Trygve talked about trees. I mean, there was a great deal more to it than that. But the heart of his message was to integrate the wisdom of Psalm 1 into our bones, and to pray that God would make us like trees. I've been working on interiorizing the text: "Happy are those who do not follow the advice of the wicked, or walk the path that sinners tread, or sit in the seat of scoffers. But their delight is in the law of the Lord, and on his law they meditate day and night. They are like trees planted by streams of water, which yield their fruit in its season, and their leaves do not either. In all that they do, they prosper" (Ps 1:1–3). *Lord, make me a tree.*

I've already gone on so long, but I want to tell you about Tuesday. Several of us went on a hike to Columbia Falls. It was the kind of hike that makes me wish I lived anywhere but Illinois—challenging elevation, gorgeous vistas, waterfall created by the Creator and not some well-intentioned but ecologically godawful dam. On the way up the mountain, members of the cohort took turns reciting Scriptures. To get to the waterfall we had to scramble alongside the creek for a couple hundred feet. When we arrived at the falls, Andy turned a branch into an aspergillum and led us in a liturgy of remembering our baptisms. The cold water felt so good and holy on my face I let out a joyous whoop (which is, I suspect, *so* Katherine). When we'd come down from the mountain I saw that Benjamin and his stepmom had both texted me the link to Ed's obituary. Winn encouraged me to read it aloud to the four of us in the car. I did, and the moment I looked up, I saw a billboard for A&W root beer. The last time I had a root beer float I was with Ed; we'd talked about them after going to an old-timey state fair, complete with a flea circus. We decided we'd eat them every time we were together. I could hardly get the words out. I was so stunned by the providential timing. So we stopped for floats and toasted Ed. So good, and so holy.

And then, Tuesday night. I suspect this is one of those stories that one tells only to hear, "Well, I guess you had to be there." But it was a night, Devon. Andy, Dan, Jonathan, Trygve, Winn, Eric, and I were sitting around a fire in the Petersons' backyard—Selah House, as they called it. I had my heart set on praying the Northumbria Evening Prayer, so we pulled it up on our cell phones and prayed together. Praying just makes me want to pray more. Well, drinking Sip N' Go Naked from Tamarack Brewery just makes me want to drink more, and I did drink more than I usually do. I was tipsy on the apricot wheat beer when I noticed myself quietly discharging a burp. And before I know it I am telling them about how I was in Latin Club when I was in high school, and how I was the undefeated champion at the Latin Club Burping Contest held at our annual Saturnalia Celebration, and how no one expected the quiet freshman to annihilate the junior football player named Pat who was the clear front-runner for that year's burping contest. And then I told them how the Latin Club participated in the annual Ohio Junior Classical League competition, and how our school was undefeated, and how our mascot was a baby-doll head named Caput and at one point I found myself sitting on the shoulders of Pat leading my fellow league members in a raucous chant: "Give me a C! Give me an A! . . ." I should add that at some point during the telling of these ridiculous yet true stories that I let out a massive belch. *Massive* belch. And I had them laughing so hard that Trygve got up, walked away, and bent over double, scarcely able to breathe. I want to believe that this, too, was good and holy. It was certainly Katherine being Katherine, and all the multitudes I contain. (I am remembering the look on your face when you learned that I love rap and hip hop.) Of course, the next day I felt sheepish, and worried that I'd annoyed everyone with my drunk girl antics. They tell me this is not the case. Christ plays in ten thousand places.

Now I must decide how ambitious for Jesus I am this week: am I going to memorize the Pentecost story, or am I not?

I hope you are well, dear Devon, despite the seams of ore that are your sorrow. Tell me what you love about *My Bright Abyss*, will you?

Peace,
Katherine

June 4, 2022

Dear Katherine,

 I wrote you a long, angry letter about violence, but I've decided not to send it. It started with my own history of it, but by the end of it I was blaming God for modeling it for us. I don't know that I'm wrong, but something about the blame rings hollow to me. I have a problem with authority—I've been accused of that by several authority figures, and it's the truth—and there's something combative in me that wants to challenge the powers that be. I wonder if it was always God I was picking a fight with, in all those moments of impudence with parents, employers, and supervisors. I don't know if I'm wrong, wanting to hold God accountable for some of our sins, but I know my logic feels incomplete and too human to stand on its own. Maybe one day I'll hit upon something more inspired, but for now I'd rather respond to your beautiful letter.

 I'm not sure there's such a thing as an uncomplicated emotion of any kind, unless you're God. God's feelings are pure. I also don't believe in happiness, at least not as a state of being. Whose life is "happy"? "Happy" occurs, but in moments, not lifetimes. As we said, life has too many complexities.

 Montana, though, sounds like it was full of joy. A Katherine kind of joy, and I'm so grateful you were there as Ed's life was ending. I still think it was the best thing. For the record, the "Katherine the Great Burping Champion" was soooo not a "you had to be there" story, and I'm glad you brought me into it. It was so good to meet the Katherine who out-belched a football player. It makes all the sense in the world that she's a part of you, and I hope she still gets out and about these days. It seems like she would be a great and fearless leader to the part that categorizes your hilarious storytelling as drunk antics. Maybe the former could convince the latter that there's nothing wrong with occasionally getting too tipsy in the company of dear and trusted colleagues, and now friends. Nevertheless, you are so very, irrepressibly Katherine, and it's one of the best things about you. I don't think you could hide yourself if you tried, and the way you inhabit yourself encourages me to do the same. I am not and never will be a belcher, but I am not always (often?) cute, or "chill," or easy, and I'm beginning to forgive myself for it.

 Truly I tell you, you have helped me come into myself. My real self, which was always there, but buried beneath affectations and beliefs that others handed me, and compressed under layer upon layer of coping strategies. So much of what I professed to value was nothing but vapor (speaking of Ecclesiastes), but I am sorting myself now. In *Confessions*, Augustine reflects on his lust, noticing, "From bad choices an urge arises; and the urge, yielded to, because a compulsion; and the compulsion, unresisted, becomes slavery."[1] *Confessions* was the first theology I read, and it hit me at the center of my dysfunction. My life had become a mosaic of bad choices that eventually enslaved me, but I make different choices now. Wiman writes, "Every man has a man within him that must die,"[2] but I don't believe that's possible. The woman in me who leaned into chaos and worshiped at the shrine of individualism I now disavow still lives within me. She is there, and some nights I feel like I have to chain her to the bed to keep myself safe. I feel her stirring, and I take to the streets to walk her out of my system, to lull her to sleep with the rhythm of my feet scraping the sidewalk. I'm afraid of her, but when I named that terror both you and Ian quoted the same Scripture: "Perfect love drives out fear" (1 John 4:18 NIV). I think about that now when I'm suffering and tempted to throw all this work out the window, and it helps. It doesn't cast out fear, not entirely, but it helps me feel safer. I trust in God. I really do. For what? Not sure. I don't know what it means that he will provide, but I believe it.

I don't judge you for a second for how much you love your brothers. Not only because I would never describe my own theology as "liberal"—I'm annoyed that "liberal" and "conservative" should apply to theology in the sense of social values, because I don't know if the politicization maps on so seamlessly—but because I don't believe in rejection based on differences. In this climate of intolerance for intolerance, I'm a radical. We're called to love our neighbor, and our neighbor doesn't always live how we live. Kierkegaard responds to Corinthians, "Love seeks not its own," and challenges that to love others for their similarities to us is not love, but "preference."[3] We want friends who vote how we vote and family who parrot our opinions, and we would trade love for the lazy comfort of congeniality. Loving for similarity is loving what we see in the mirror, and that is vanity. Love—real love—is anything but vanity.

Ian tests that precept. I don't think I've told you that he's the last person I would describe as "liberal." He's orthodox in his beliefs and in the

1. Augustine, *Confessions*, 168.
2. Wiman, *My Bright Abyss*, 132.
3. Kierkegaard, *Works of Love*, 284.

church's teachings, so you can imagine on which matters we might clash. And we do clash. I didn't mention this out of loyalty to him, because I want to protect him from judgment, but we got into it the other night about women's inclusion in the priesthood. I can't call it an argument exactly, he wasn't lobbying for exclusion, but he contextualized it pretty easily. Something about women's subordination to men stemming from Genesis and the punishment for sin: men are doomed to break their bodies, and women to desire and serve their husbands, etc. He was clear in his belief that God intended men and women to care for the world together, as equal partners, and dropped his detached philosophizing in favor of a plainspoken "no, never" when I suggested he would endorse a power dynamic if we ever married, but I questioned our compatibility. It's laughable, considering the trials that all but characterize our strange relationship, but for a second I wondered, "Is *this* going to be my line?" It wasn't and it wouldn't have been, because it's too late for me to reject him on the basis of a belief. I already love him. All of him. I didn't lie when I said we didn't argue, but I had no idea he felt that way, and learning he did knocked me sideways. I cannot help but love him, but I don't know what to do with this information. I don't know what to do with what feels like a slap in the face, but I know I won't leave him for it. If I abandon him it won't be for something like this. Love seeks not its own, "For the true lover does not love his own individuality. He rather loves each human being according to the other's individuality. But for the other person 'his own personality' is precisely 'his own,' and consequently the lover does not seek his own; quite the opposite, in others he loves 'their own.'"[4]

I'll end there. I was going to plow on into "family," "familiar," and "tradition," but there is a voice lesson to attend and axes to throw. I know you aren't well, but you are no less loved by me for it.

With the aforementioned love,
Devon

---

4. Kierkegaard, *Works of Love*, 252.

June 6, 2022

Dear Devon,

 There were axes to throw, and we threw them! As I predicted, it was a gas—even though it did trigger an unexpected discomfort in me. I felt both thrilled and repulsed by the violence of hurling sharp objects at targets. I do want to read your words about violence, if and when you are ready to share them. When I was in seminary (the first time around) I considered myself a pacifist. The US was newly at war with Afghanistan and Iraq, and I rejected both the political and theological justifications for state violence. I was obsessed with Dietrich Bonhoeffer, a German pastor who was arrested and killed for his part in a plot to assassinate Hitler. He participated in the attempt even though he did not believe that it is ever appropriate for a Christian to engage in harm—even when the intended victim is one so evil as Hitler. He did what he did and threw himself upon the mercy of God—not to continue in sin in order that grace may increase, but because he couldn't personally justify preferring his own holiness over the possibility of saving people from the murderous chancellor. I think that was what moved me most about Bonhoeffer. As I've acknowledged to you before, I was a bit insufferable in my youth, and I was most unbearable about my high-minded principles. We've talked about the violence in the Bible—I railed against that violence as histrionically as I protested the wars. The first sermon I ever preached was about Jephthah's daughter. It was before I really understood that no matter what, the responsibility of a preacher is to be faithful to the gospel—to listen deeply enough to the words and the Word to find and proclaim some good news. I just raged about the horrors of violence in the Bible. I wanted to excise the unacceptable bits from the holy Scriptures. Like, Psalm 137 should end after verse 6. There is no need to lift up imprecatory prayers, no need to imagine the skulls of enemy infants split by jagged rocks. I still detest violence, especially within myself; even the innocuous aggression of axe-throwing quickened my shame. But I am old enough to understand now that it doesn't actually help anything to pretend it away, old enough to appreciate that one of the reasons the Bible holds its own through the centuries is because it is so brutally honest about the nature of humankind. Our capacity for foolishness and faithfulness, for selfishness and soulfulness. Our ability to love, and our ability to hate. There is violence in me and there is violence in Scripture and rather than rage I am cultivating repentance. That being said, I am also old enough to understand that there are contexts in which violence is, if not good, nevertheless necessary.

I appreciate your impulse to protect Ian. Maybe I needed not to know, at least for a while, that he doesn't affirm women in ministry. I don't feel judgment toward him but I do feel something. I also felt it when you told me you were talking to the associate pastor at the Presbyterian church that doesn't ordain women or affirm LGBTQ+ people. And when a friend—not a close friend, but a person I nonetheless respect and care for—joined the Catholic Church. I feel anxious and sad and threatened. Defensive. In theory, I want to be able to build relationships that transcend differences. And I do! But some differences are, well, different. My ordination is so vital to my identity I wince to consider that for so many people it is at best a benign misconception and at worst a diabolical sham. It makes me feel childish, like I'm on the verge of throwing a tantrum and stamping my foot. Why do I feel such a need to defend myself? I've felt it with atheists, too. *Just because you don't believe women can be pastors doesn't mean I'm not a real pastor!* (Stamps foot.) *Just because you don't believe in God doesn't mean God isn't real!* (Stamps foot.) I still have some growing up to do, Devon. My insecurity is tiresome. I want to trust God, and not give a shit about what other people think.

I love that you trust God even though you're not sure what for. It reminds me of the art I have on my wall, the watercolor painting of my favorite Buechner quote. I'm sure you've seen it when you've borrowed my office for therapy sessions. "Here is the world. Beautiful and terrible things will happen. Don't be afraid."[1] There is a quote within the quote, of course. Buechner echoes the words whispered to terrified souls throughout holy Scripture. *Do not be afraid*, God says to Abraham, to Hagar, to Joseph, to Moses. *Do not be afraid*, Moses says to the Hebrew people. *Do not be afraid*, the angel says to Zechariah, to Mary, to Joseph. *Do not be afraid*, Jesus says to his disciples—more times than you can count on both hands.

I love that Buechner quote, but I also despise it. I love the promise that beautiful things will happen. I hate the reminder that terrible things will happen. If it were up to me, it would go like this: *Here is the world. Nothing bad will ever happen to you. Do not be afraid.* That makes more sense, right? That the reason we need not fear is because there's nothing to be afraid of. But that's pretty much the exact opposite of what Buechner means, and what Scripture reveals.

---

1. Buechner, *Wishful Thinking*, 34.

Love Letters to God

"Who will separate us from the love of Christ?" Paul asks. "Will hardship, or distress, or persecution, or famine, or nakedness, or peril, or sword?" (Rom 8:38–39 NRSV). The answer is no, of course. None of these things will separate us from the love of Christ. But neither will the love of Christ separate us from these things. There is absolutely no promise that we will be spared hardship, distress, persecution, famine, nakedness, peril, or sword. I really wish we had that promise. But I will take what I can get. I suspect trust is sedimentary in nature, built layer by layer over time. I hope you can hear this and let it be another layer in your trust in God: the woman inside you cannot separate you from the love of Christ. Not her trauma, not her violence. Not her lust, not her idolatry, not her fear, not her rage. I'm glad you're declining Wiman's invitation to let her die. I'm glad you have compassion for her. I understand what he means but I also think there's another way that is still faithful. It really is about love. Your love for her. God's love for her. I do not know her but I think I love her, too. I certainly love my friend Devon, with all her intensity.

To be clear, I am entirely with you on the liberal/conservative thing. It's exhausting, the way the church has just mimicked the divisions of the culture. Despite the fact that Jesus prayed *at length* that the church would be one. And yet, out of laziness I claim the labels. It's all relative. When I am at school, I am liberal. When I am at church or among my clergy friends, I am conservative. Meanwhile, I just want more of the God revealed in Jesus Christ. I started reading Henri Nouwen's book *Letters to Marc About Jesus*, because apparently there's no such thing as too many epistles in my life. He writes, "At one time I was so immersed in problems of church and society that my whole life had become a sort of drawn-out, wearisome discussion. Jesus had been pushed into the background; he had himself become just another problem. Fortunately, it hasn't stayed that way. Jesus has stepped out in the front again and asked me, 'And you, who do you say that I am?' It has become clearer to me than ever that my personal relationship with Jesus is the heart of my existence."[2] This is what I want for the second half of my life: an ever-deepening friendship with Jesus.

These letters are a part of that. Thank you, as always, for continuing this sacred correspondence.

In Christ,
Katherine

---

2. Nouwen, *Letters to Marc About Jesus*, 14.

June 8, 2022

Dear Katherine,

We are so different. Not in all ways—sometimes when we sit across from each other over breakfast, it feels like conversing with myself—but in some, like in our relationship with violence. You told me later that it unnerved you, but I didn't feel an ounce of your revulsion; axe-throwing thrilled me. It was written all over my face in those photos so I doubt you missed it, but I felt exuberant. Elated. I pranced out of the axe-throwing place and soared through the rest of my day. Throwing those axes, hearing the subtle thwack in the wood when I landed one, and even, God forgive me, realizing out loud my capacity to hurt another human should I need to, made me feel alive. Maybe I'm imagining it, but I was sure I caught you in a brief moment of horror as you heard me exclaim that. I want to try and explain this.

[The author has redacted the following sections due to personal content, which she has chosen to keep private. Please read on below.]

Do not be afraid, do not be afraid, do not be afraid . . .
It wasn't until I found myself alone at midnight on my next birthday, sobbing and alone and trying to muster up the courage to really hurt myself, that I understood: violence is violence and it is dangerous. I'm dangerous.

I've sweat clean through my thin cotton dress in the writing of this. I needed you to see that I'm a perpetrator, because I know your fierce love for me and how you would weep for me as the object of violence. I need you to know that I'm the subject as well, because that might change how you feel. I've been a monster, Katherine, and it doesn't feel right accepting your compassion without you knowing that.

I've written you this letter three times now, because with each iteration I get closer to some kind of truth. Last time I unleashed my fury on God, and for how his unspeakable violence against humanity created a template for us to follow. Maybe I didn't want to blame my father or my brother, because they came by it honestly and they're trying to love better than before. Maybe I didn't want to take full accountability for my own lethality, as though another explanation might so remove me from the origin of my violence that I could tolerate my past. I reject the psalm that raves, "Happy is the one who seizes your infants and dashes them against the rocks" (Ps 137:9 NIV), and the version of God who condoned the psalmist's vision. The same God who dispatched his only son to suffer and die as a human, for humans, is the God who commanded that the tribes "utterly destroy" any number of unchosen civilizations. Yes, I know they were corrupting influences, but I don't much care. Our God demanded slaughter and genocide and I don't know that I can ever accept that.

What I can do is see God through a clinical lens. He's the father who had kids too young and couldn't manage to parent responsibly. It was his first go-around. He didn't know what he was doing. He learned, though. After centuries of his chosen people rejecting him and persisting in their foolish ways, he tried a different tactic. He always loved us, but he couldn't figure out how to reach us until he determined to suffer alongside us, and to die an agonizing death in exchange for our salvation. Violence there as well, but at least the kind meant to extinguish the forces of evil.

Christianity wouldn't be without Christ, and however obvious that is I'm saying it because Christ signifies a difference in how God understood love. Or maybe it signifies the point at which God understood that humans needed to be loved in a different kind of way. He loved us the whole time, but he wasn't getting through to us. Is that the fault of humans? Sure. Definitely. How many times did we spit on his grace? Nevertheless, God had one tool in his tool belt—a hammer—and everywhere he saw nails. Jesus, a carpenter, had many tools at his disposal, and he was a hell of a lot more effective in helping people understand love.

I think God made some mistakes, and I also think that when we start questioning God's infallibility we can unravel the fabric of dogma that holds Christianity together, and I don't want this. You know I love the binding. It's only that I can't divorce our violence from his. Maybe I'll get there one day.

The last thing I want to impart is that I still love God. Desperately. I love him with the same animal intensity I unleashed on my brother. I love him no matter what I believe he has done wrong—like my brother, my father, myself—and questioning him doesn't make a dent in that. At least not for me. I hope he can understand. I hope you can understand.

With love, and fear, and trembling,
Devon

June 10, 2022

Dear Katherine,

Another sleepless night. I've had the "have you tried" conversation for decades with any number of well-meaning people, but my body seems intent on disrupting its own rest. I am so tired. I can manage that after thirty-five years of practice, but it troubles me to feel my brain power slip away as the day goes on. To reach the hour at which I start to clutch at lucidity and the present moment blurs at the edges. This is a problem, for a therapist. It is especially a problem for a therapist like me, whose work relies on presence and who expects to give the best of herself to her clients, which I think is fair considering my hourly rate. I melt with gratitude when I close my laptop after the last session of the day. Not because I'm tired of clients, but because my eyes don't have to strain with the effort of tracking micro-expressions, and my mind can rest from the dance my mind choreographs anew to partner with each unique nervous system. I am so tired, but I have mornings now, and I can use them for things like this.

This isn't what kept me up last night, but I'm having a minor reckoning with myself and my beliefs about inclusivity in the church. I had such a good talk with that Presbyterian pastor. In my youth I never mastered the art of disagreeing without morphing into a high-minded, insufferable little goblin, but it came so easily on Tuesday. I had no problem informing the pastor that I disagreed with his church's stance on women's ordination and restrictions around marriage, and we went on to have the most respectful and curious conversation, free from expectation that the other would change their mind. We listened to each other. He validated my discomfort that his church bars women from the priesthood, but said Scripture to him suggests that God intended the priestly class to be men. He had a similar take on gay marriage, but his disagreement didn't bother me because he treated my opinions as credible and worthy of attention. The secular general public has this idea that all Christians proselytize and bring the hammer with their dogma, but that couldn't be further from the case with this pastor, or anyone else I've met at this church.

Regarding our differences, we'll never know who's more right, because while divinely inspired, the Bible leaves room for interpretation. We don't stone people anymore. We don't cast out "unclean" people from the community—we don't really believe in "unclean" people—and salvation is for everyone these days. Hallelujah! We keep a biblical worldview, but in any number of ways we have reevaluated practices that don't fit like they did a millennia ago. The church probably wouldn't retain too many women if we had to live under threat of stoning and under the yoke of our husbands (a generalization, because I know not all Christians have adapted the latter). The point is that we have always cherry-picked the Bible in some way or another, and "It said so in [insert book here]" isn't the most stalwart defense. Even the orthodox amongst us make choices about which parts of Scripture to elevate, and excluding women is a choice. Refusing to sanctify more than one kind of marriage is a choice.

To varying degrees, I'm uncomfortable with these choices. I said before that I don't really care that others hold these opinions, because I don't believe in their validity and I doubt Jesus would, but what would it mean to affiliate myself with a church that endorses what I denounce? I could never in good conscience ask certain friends of mine to accompany me to worship, knowing that my church would withhold sacraments. I wouldn't feel right inviting you, either, who has endured the patronizing skepticism and rejection of your ordination. How could I look my queer clients in the face, and out of one side of my mouth preach love, while out the other side scramble to come up with a good-enough explanation for why I worship somewhere that tells them their love is meant to be "worked through" and not celebrated? It feels like betrayal.

And what about the person in my life, the person I love, whose doctrinal mind works like the Presbyterian pastor's?

This conflict inconveniences me. It would be so nice to walk down the block and into that big, beautiful church, insulated with stained glass and ringing with the more traditional hymns I treasure. I've met people my age there, too. Bright, thoughtful, funny people who parse Scripture while they drink wine and munch on a Mariano's meat and cheese plate. I have exactly two people who fit this description in my life—you are one of them—and I long for more. It would be so convenient to set up shop and build community in my literal community. I don't want to keep starting over, but I'm worried I'll have to.

There's no tidy conclusion to this letter, or this dilemma. Perhaps we can talk more on Monday, when we have lattes (lavender?!) to take the edge off.

Until then,
Devon

June 10, 2022

Dear Devon,

I am going to keep this response brief and only to your last letter, and circle back to respond to your holy yet harrowing second-to-last letter with undivided attention and sufficient time. This is what I think you should do about your dilemma with the church: go to the Presbyterian church in your neighborhood. Really. It isn't healthy, the way that churches have sequestered themselves into hives of like-minded subcultures. Nor is it healthy to "church shop," as if trying on congregations were akin to trying on jeans. Congregations are not consumer products; congregation is the collective noun describing a group of souls. And souls do best when they stay local; when they know and love their neighbors. "The Word became flesh and blood and moved into the neighborhood," as Eugene translated it (John 1:14 MSG). Speaking of Eugene, his wisdom was what popped into my mind when I read your letter this morning. From his conversation with Krista Tippett on *On Being*:

> **PETERSON:** Go to the closest church where you live and the smallest. After six months, if it isn't working, go find the next smallest church.
>
> **TIPPET:** *What is it about small rather than big?*
>
> **PETERSON:** Because you have to deal with people as they are. You've got to learn how to love them when they are not loveable.[1]

Maybe the Presbyterian church in your neighborhood isn't the smallest, but it is in your neighborhood. It isn't perfect, but it has bright, thoughtful, and funny people who like charcuterie and love Jesus. Learn to love them when their convictions about women and LGBTQ+ people aren't lovable.

Maybe the better counsel would be to pray about it, rather than tell you to go there. So, I take it back: pray about it. Remember that because the Scriptures really can be interpreted to support a variety of worldviews, we truly must depend upon the fellowship of the Holy Spirit to be our guide. And know that if you discern that you are called to affiliate with your neighborhood Presbyterian church, you have the blessing of the Rev. Katherine Willis Pershey.

---

1. Peterson, "Answering God."

More soon, my friend. I am holding you in my heart with great tenderness and love. Oh, how I hope you can get some rest.

Peace,
Katherine
P.S. The insufferable little goblin in me sees, honors, and is grateful for the insufferable little goblin in you.

June 15, 2022

Dear Devon,

First, let me reiterate what you already know but I need you to hear, again: I love you.

And I do weep for you. I weep for your pain; the pain you endured, and the pain you caused. I weep for the fear that still clutches at your soul even though Jesus is trying so damn hard to cast it all out with his perfect love. His perfect love for you. Yes, I love you fiercely—but my love is pale and insubstantial compared to the love of God. You might know that on an intellectual level—we did, after all, read *The Love That Is God* together—but I am praying that you know this in your body and mind and soul. Your body and mind and soul that have been broken, but by the grace of God can be made whole.

As I read your letter—the first version a few days ago, and the revised one just this afternoon—I feel deeply conscious of the insufficiency of words, and the insufficiency of—well, me. My old anxieties about saying the right thing aren't even bothering to kick in. I am at least wise enough to now know that there is no right thing. (Even though you have reassured me you are hard to offend, I still know there are a great many wrong things to utter.) I have even fleetingly questioned the wisdom of this whole project—as I have said to you before, the last thing I would ever want to do is use or exploit our relationship for the sake of my doctor of ministry project. But you trust me, and I trust that you trust me, and I trust you. As we confirmed on Monday, ours is a providential friendship, a covenantal friendship. Maybe the only reason this can work is because the project is so secondary to the mutual ministry of these letters.

Look at me, prattling on, in a paragraph that started with the insufficiency of words. I don't think I am stalling, exactly. I was last week, when I read the first version, because I desperately needed my first response to this letter to be embodied. I needed to greet you with arms wide open, embracing you with the ferocity of a holy righteous bear. I needed to grasp your hands in mine, because we know that human touch can be sacramental, invoking the very presence and blessing of God.

But now I have hugged you, and I have reached around extra hot lavender lattes to squeeze your hand, and I have read this fuller version. I wrongly assumed you were going to redact. Instead you expanded, giving new depth to that old cliché "brutally honest." You were honest about brutality: done to you, and done by you. It is one thing to peel off the bandages and show a friend one's wounds. It is another thing entirely to reveal one's shame. I feel like there's often an edge to that compliment *you're so brave.* Like, there's a subtext implying foolishness. Devon, you are not a fool. Your courage astonishes me. Your trust humbles me. And because you were honest with me, I must be honest with you. I am overwhelmed, but not in the way you might expect (or fear, for that matter). I am not overwhelmed by a "trauma dump," as you fretted via text. I did not experience these letters as emotional unloading. I did not, and do not, feel burdened.

I am overwhelmed by sorrow, empathy, and love. And I'm overwhelmed by something I'm struggling to name. It is not judgment or justification. It is not pity or fear. Even as I reject your claim that you've been a monster, I will not do you the disservice of pretending you were without sin. It pisses me off when friends are unwilling to shake their heads at one another's transgressions. To be clear, I am also not without sin. I want you to shake your head at my transgressions. Am I able to thread that needle of concurring that terrible wrong was done to you and by you without layering even an ounce of added shame? I do not want to shame you, friend. I feel, rather unexpectedly, like a priest. I feel as though I have received your confession. And I feel as though I have the honor of echoing the absolution of your sins. I am too Protestant to believe I could ever be the absolver. But please receive this assurance of pardon just as humbly as I have received your confession: Devon, by the grace of God you are forgiven. I am overwhelmed with confidence that nothing can separate you from the love of God in Jesus Christ. Nothing. God has already forgiven you as unequivocally as the Father raced out to welcome the Prodigal Son back into the household of grace. Kill the fatted calf. *This daughter of mine was dead and is alive again; she was lost and is found!*

By the grace of God I hope you are healed, too, or at least healing. Nothing can separate you from the love of God in Christ—not sin, and not trauma. I guess I am still feeling the priestly vibes because I am imagining anointing your forehead with oil and praying for the healing of your body, mind, and soul.

I am also imagining baptizing you in the name of the Father and of the Son and of the Holy Spirit, and submerging you in the waters of Lake Michigan and watching you rise into your new life in Christ.

And now, a hard left turn: maybe you thought I was going to clutch my pearls about the [redacted] (okay, maybe I did, a little, but that's fair?). But I got *real* pearl-clutchy about the way you are interpreting Scripture—and more pointedly, the way you are conceiving of God. I take the Bible very seriously but I do not take it literally. I believe those passages describing a violent God are not indicative of a violent God who is just too immature to behave as a properly gracious deity. I believe they reflect an incomplete and inaccurate human perspective on God. Considering the extreme violence inherent to many ancient religious mythologies, it's a wonder the Old Testament presents a God who creates with a Word and not a war. The Babylonian creation myth has the goddess Tiamat torn asunder by Marduk, who establishes the earth and heavens with the parts of her bloodied body. Meanwhile, we have ancient poetry celebrating that God is slow to anger and abounding in steadfast love. Yes, we also have ancient poetry expressing prayers of violence—but I can't reject the last verse of Psalm 137 anymore, precisely because I *don't* believe there is a version of God who condones it. God will listen to our angriest prayers, but the whole sweep of Scripture makes it abundantly clear to me that God condemns the acting out of our angriest prayers. The Bible is violent because human beings are violent—this is true in the Old and New Testaments. After all, it is human beings who nail Christ to the cross. They reject God. They *kill* God. I should say *we* reject and kill God, for I truly do believe that story has universal, even cosmic consequences. But Devon, if we truly believe that Jesus is the Son of God, that "he is the reflection of God's glory and the exact imprint of God's very being" (Heb 1:3 NRSV), we cannot for a moment believe that God is violent. There is nothing violent about Jesus. He is wise and gentle, merciful and holy. He *is* love. And his death on the cross is, to me, the ultimate repudiation of violence—divine or human. Life triumphs over death. Love over hate. Vulnerability over violence. There are so many different ways to interpret everything that happens on the cross, but for me it all comes down to love.

I know you are committed to reading the Bible in its entirety but sometimes I worry about how much time that means dwelling on incomplete revelations of the heart of God. As for me, I'm still reading the first psalm day after day, and meditating on the law of the Lord: to love God with all my heart and soul and strength, and to love my neighbor as myself. I want to be like a tree planted by streams of water, my roots reaching deep into the Ground of all Being, the Source of Life. The God of Love.

This letter is incomplete. There is so much more to say. But I will not make you wait on my response any longer, and the conversation will continue in due time.

Love,
Katherine

June 16, 2022

Dear Katherine,

   I knew you'd recoil at my all-too-emotional interpretation of Scripture, and in a way that's why I included it.

   Children need limits to help them understand where they end and something else begins, and boundaries to bump up against that won't imprison but contain them. I didn't always have those limits, and in some ways I've moved through the world like an unruly, undisciplined child, rejecting rules I can't make sense of and rebelling against authority so instinctively that the ensuing discipline shocks me. Nevertheless, "I yearn to belong to something, to be contained by an all-embracing mind that sees me as a single thing."[1] I welcome binding when I choose it, and I choose Christianity. I also choose you as not only a friend but a guide, and the security in our relationship makes it safe for me to push boundaries. In the years when I struggled to find an audience, I censored myself out of essays for fear of what might come back at me, but I'm genuinely curious about what will come back to me when I'm brutally honest with you. I don't mean to provoke, but your strong reactions help me understand mine, and corral the wildness in me. It's unlikely it will tame it, and I don't think I'd want it to, but I am someone who feels a LOT. I am also someone who won't temper her emotional responses to Scripture, because they're important, and because the Bible is not a textbook; it is rife with feeling and personal relevance and provocation. That said, I also process in phases. I need to feel before filtering those emotions through a more scholarly, dispassionate lens, but I am nothing if not a student and will always return there. If I haven't articulated this clearly enough, or if my emotions deceived you into thinking otherwise, please trust that I know that I'm in process. I know I'm at the beginning of a journey with God and with Scripture, and none of my opinions feel solid right now. I don't need them to be and frankly I don't think they can be, at this point.

   Please also trust that I trust in the love of God that is relentless and unconditional and eternal. I trust in this because I *feel* it, and not because I read something somewhere. You see, my feelings aren't only in service of rebellion.

   Nevertheless, I still can't deny the presence of violence. I know that the civilizations annihilated were wicked and corrupt, and if they were

---

1. Rilke, *Book of Hours*, 139.

thoroughly abominable, a scourge on love, and a threat to God's chosen people, I can better understand their destruction. But it still was destruction, wasn't it? I'm in the middle of Revelation, and that book terrifies me. I know the end-times are part of righting the world and liberating it from chaos, but it sounds utterly terrifying. I'm not trying to be obstinate—however many times I need to assure you that I *know* I'm learning, I will—but I'm stuck. I know God is love. I know that. I really, really do. And I'm not angry with him like my last letter implied. I didn't know it at the time, but I see now how my feelings overpowered my ability to hold something uncomfortable. As I said, Scripture trembles with emotion and I need my feelings, but they cannot be the only lens through which I understand our faith. I'm committed to understanding the violence precisely because I trust in God, but I still see violence and I'm starting to feel lost that I can't see otherwise. Not because I believe God is violent and that dismays me, but because I'm not getting something that everyone else seems to grasp. I'm flustered and floundering to explain the nuance of my feelings, and realizing that when I write uninhibitedly, I set myself up to be misunderstood. To me, they're thoughts and feelings subject to change and grow, but they're so forceful that they don't land that way. Everything I say sounds certain. Remember my first letter? When I told you how Eric uncharitably called me a "force"? I feel the detriment of that now.

But enough about me. I want to thank you for how you responded to that wild letter. You may be too Protestant to see yourself as an absolver, but I am not too Protestant to accept your absolution. I badly needed you to see my sin, and to not soothe away that I have also done wrong. Thank you for letting me be a whole person, and showing me the respect of acknowledging the whole truth. I want to be loved in spite of my sin, and not for a delusional purity that none of us possess. I want to be known for my depravity and accepted anyway. God does this and you did this. I regret the brevity of this paragraph for fear it undermines the depths of my gratitude, but there's nothing more to say than thank you for loving me, thank you for using your priestly powers (kidding, kidding) to absolve me, and thank you for your prayers of healing. You brought me peace.

This letter feels incomplete. I'm stifling the urgency to explain myself to death, but what that tells me is that this is a conversation to resume over lattes.

Until lattes,
Devon

June 17, 2022

Dear Katherine,

I am at long last in the air, flying to Brooklyn. Or I guess Queens, because that's the borough in which LaGuardia makes its home, but I am Brooklyn bound. Flying frightens me, and flying during a storm is almost more than I can handle, so I've enlisted everyone I can to pray for safety. I must have used the prayer hands emoji half a dozen times already, and not only with my Christian friends. It felt oddly liberating to drop the word "prayer" into texts with secular folk, when once a claim to faith wracked me with anxiety. Now, I am at ease. Those who love me seem accepting of my conversion, or at least indifferent enough that they don't care.

Maybe it's that we made it into the air today, or maybe it's having listened to Father Mike's assurances that getting to know our faith does not happen all at once (remember the nonviolence that I persist in understanding as violence?) but I want to write about hope. I have it for the first time, and in abundance. Maybe that comes as a surprise after the last letter spiraled into anxiety so destabilizing it surprised even myself, but I do have it. At the beginning of the pandemic, Ian lent me the book I mentioned today via text, *Hope in Time of Abandonment*, and it hit me so forcefully that it launched me ten steps closer to God. I won't pretend to understand all that Jacques Ellul wrote, but in his closing pages he seems to define hope, in part, as the thing we hold to when we have no reason to hope. He implies that real hope, not "I hope it doesn't rain today," or "I hope you have a nice day!" corresponds to moments of abject futility. That kind of hope is irrational without faith, but with it, we can endure. Ellul's hope, Christian hope, has not to do with wish, but with a promise. I read that, and all of a sudden I had something to hold on to. It was more than a gift—it was a blessing—but in moments I've wondered if it's also a delusion.

I met a new friend at the Covenant Bible study, and we went to her apartment for a drink after we put down Revelation for the night. After an hour of deflecting her questions about my personal life with my own about hers, she finally pinned me down. She had disarmed me with prosecco, so by that point I didn't stand a chance. We had spent the better part of that hour talking about her recent breakup, and she asked me if I had the kind of love in my life that she had lost. I never know what to say about Ian, so I shared only enough to convey the complicated, conflicted nature of our relationship, and in response she asked if I had prayed for God's guidance. I had prayed, I told her, but I did not know his answer because he responded with silence. As the words left my mouth, I felt and saw something in my core that I had felt and seen many times before: a bright, penetrating, terrible little light shining a hole through my chest, that emerges whenever I despair of this matter. It comes unbidden and it so diminishes the despondency that I can actually feel it shrink. I think this is hope. I also wonder if it is God. I wonder if this is how he speaks on this matter; through quiet, insistent attacks on hopelessness.

I mentioned the other day how struck I was by the passage in 1 Kings when Elijah meets God at Horeb: "He said, 'Go out and stand on the mountain before the Lord, for the Lord is about to pass by.' Now there was a great wind, so strong that it was splitting mountains and breaking rocks in pieces before the Lord, but the Lord was not in the wind; and after the wind an earthquake, but the Lord was not in the earthquake; and after the earthquake a fire, but the Lord was not in the fire." In one awesome natural disaster after another, the Lord is nowhere to be found. But then, "after the fire a sound of sheer silence" (1 Kgs 19:10–12 NRSV), and in that silence, the voice of God. This feels right to me, that God might speak in a whisper and not in a whirlwind of sound and fury—"signifying nothing,"[1] as Shakespeare might add. I've also heard him in a thunderstorm so thunderous that it shook the house, but when I heard Jesus call to me, "Daughter," it was with a voice so human and so quiet that I almost missed it. It's like my brain recorded his voice, because I can still hear it exactly as it sounded that night. Another blessing, another gift.

I don't feel anxious today and I don't feel lost in a haze of incomprehension. I am patient and at peace with myself and my young Christian mind, and I have also stocked up on podcasts and books to organize me in moments of disarray. I still don't quite get the violence, but I'm pretty sure I will.

I will miss you these next couple of weeks, but I wish you that same peace at home and on your travels, and look forward to our reunion at King Spa. There's something baptismal about meeting naked in the waters, right?

Love,
Devon

---

1. Shakespeare, *Macbeth*, 68.

July 5, 2022

Dear Devon,

 As much as I try not to start these letters with apologies, this time I really do owe you one. It's been far too long since I last responded. I can't really say where the time went. There was an overscheduled week at church, and a sorely needed family vacation on Lake Huron. And then there was our epic birthday spa day, pub crawl, and sleepover. Good Lord it was fun to spend that time with you, especially after a few weeks on divergent paths. I loved seeing your apartment, and meeting your good dog Bowie, and squealing over the extravagant gift of the Resurrection Duet. Ever since we first used that soap and lotion in the Longman & Eagle bathroom, I've been daydreaming about the scent. It's unlike anything I've ever smelled before. And it's so wildly expensive! I truly did not see that gift coming, and I am astonished by your generosity. Now I need to make sure I'm not miserly with it. I need to slather that nard on like there's no tomorrow, all the while trusting that there is.

 And that's all I have for the moment. It is altogether inadequate. But as I said via text, my heart is broken and my brain is mush. The violence in Highland Park was just too much, too close, too familiar. Today was my first day back after a week away, and I'm spent from playing catch-up. I know full well you have more to say. I do too, but it will have to wait another day. But not another twenty days! I promise.

 I love you.

Peace,
Katherine

July 5, 2022

Dear Katherine,

It took me by surprise that I feel so much about yesterday's shooting, because I usually feel numb. I'm not proud and not a little bit ashamed that I've shut off the part of me that empathizes with such tragedies, but for the most part I have. The therapist in me reminds myself and my clients that this is protective, and the therapist in me is right in this. However, the therapist in me is not all of me, and the rest of me feels a little like a monster, or if not a monster, a half-human, emotionally compromised by the world she lives in. I don't like that I don't feel much sometimes, but I'm trying to forgive my body for its survival strategy.

In any case.

I'm empty after yesterday. The proximity of the violence must have made the difference between acknowledging and feeling, because I am so sad. As I mentioned, I did a 108 sun salutations yoga practice today. I filled the only three spare hours of my day with three sets of thirty-six sun salutations, because the practice is all about love. In the first set, you're asked to focus on someone easy to love. In the next, on someone hard to love, and in the last, on yourself. The first was easy because I thought about God, but I limped through the second set, urging myself on through intrusive thoughts of anger and heartbreak. The last left me nearly delirious from the emotional exhaustion of trying to love myself. I don't want you to think I feel down about myself, because that's both untrue and not the point. Or maybe I do, in the sense that I feel the hope of last week's letter draining out of me, but I'm not at the center of this sorrow. That's important, because what I'm getting at is a loss of hope in humanity. I've felt this before, and recently, and it's hard to shake because it feels so true. Humans are miraculous and beautiful, and they're also infected with evil. I believe in the beauty and I feel it. It's just that right now, mostly what I feel is that humans are lost and God is all that can save us. That's always been true, but it feels like it's all any of us have right now.

Love,
Devon

July 6, 2022

Dear Devon,

 I hope you have found some moments to rest and pray today. Your new schedule is wise in so many ways—stack all the therapy sessions into four days, so you have three-day weekends every week!—but, when something horrific happens on a Monday it means you have an awfully long time before you can catch your breath.

 A few weeks ago you sent me a link to an episode of the BibleProject—an interview with Dan Kimball about "How (Not) to Read the Bible."[2] I have listened to that one and several more since. Their approach is so different from the approach I was taught in my liberal seminary. They repeatedly insist that "the Bible is a unified story that points to Jesus." In my theological family of origin, I'd be accused of flagrant supersessionism if I started parroting this line. I've *been* accused of casual supersessionism, even before my theology started drifting to the center. Years ago I wrote a Christmas pageant that featured the angel Gabriel and Mary visiting the prophet Isaiah, aka the Ghost of Christmas Past. A friend read the script and responded, "Woe to we the casually supersessionist!" and encouraged me to "consider the theological claims" I was making. I felt like I was being sent to my room. I don't think it's necessarily supersessionist for Christians to read the Hebrew Scriptures through the lens of Christianity. It's fairly central to the New Testament and orthodox Christianity to affirm that Jesus is the fulfillment of prophecies—to imagine, as it were, that Isaiah would be nodding and saying, yup, that's the one. It doesn't negate other interpretations of the Hebrew texts—which is to say, the way that Jewish readers who do not see a Messiah in Jesus would interpret Scripture. I've thought a lot about this ever since there was a dust-up about the *Jesus Storybook Bible* among a group of liberal clergy colleagues. Someone roundly panned it because of its claim that "every story whispers Jesus' name"—including the Old Testament ones. Of course every story whispers his name—if his name is on your mind and in your heart, if his name is what you're looking for. It's like finding cruciform narratives in literature and current events and such. I guess I think postmodernity allows for multiple narratives and truth claims to exist in tension.

---

2. Mackie et al., BibleProject.

I digress. (I'm beginning to think that would be an appropriate subtitle for this project—*Love Letters to God: I Digress*.) What really threw me about that first podcast episode wasn't their eagerness to see Jesus everywhere in Scripture. It was the ease with which they dismissed the very argument I just lobbed at you a couple letters ago: *I believe those passages describing a violent God are not indicative of a violent God who is just too immature to behave as a properly gracious deity. I believe they reflect an incomplete and inaccurate human perspective on God.* They quickly concurred that interpretations such as these are just not acceptable—that the whole thing kind of falls apart if you do not assent to the notion that what the Bible says about God is fundamentally true. Perhaps *metaphorically* true, depending on the genre. But they utterly rejected the idea that parts of the Bible reflect wrongheaded human attitudes about God. I've just never really been challenged to see Scripture as authoritative. Even as a preacher. I've unapologetically cherry-picked my way through the Bible, and I'm not sure if I can keep this up. But I'm also not sure I can handle the alternative: a God who demanded slaughter and genocide. Or a God who would condemn a gay kid.

Maybe this is why I've often favored spiritual practices, theological reflection, and gospel music over biblical study. Which isn't to say I don't read or wrestle with Scripture at all. But I'm a dabbler and I will shrug and claim "different context" when I run into something uncomfortable. When I trip on something with which I do not agree. It is so much easier for me to blame humans for all the violence and evil. I wholeheartedly agree that humans are lost and God is all that can save us now. I said as much in my sermon on Sunday. But maybe I need to stop squeezing God into safe and tidy parameters.

I'm going to stop, and listen for God in the sheer silence. (Well, the relative silence. Genevieve is having a sleepover and they're watching *Free Guy* at a decent volume, and my passive-aggressive offer to fetch a nail file for Benjamin did not land, so I am still hearing the sound of my beloved biting his nails.)

More soon—on hope. And joy.

Peace,
Katherine

JULY 10, 2022

Dear Katherine,

    I still haven't caught my breath. Life right now feels like a wheezing sprint from one task to another, one suburb to another, and the whirlwind of it all has somewhat carried me away from God. I've been noticing lately how distractible I am, and I don't love it. It's fatigue, but it's also preoccupation with fraught relationships and stalled parts of my life. I give it too much attention. In *The Inner Voice of Love*, Nouwen urges himself to "understand the limitations of others." He says, "You keep listening to those who seem to reject you. But they never speak about *you*. They speak about their own limitations. They confess their poverty in the face of your needs and desires. . . . The sadness is that you perceive their necessary withdrawal as a rejection of you instead of as a call to return home and discover there your true belovedness."[1] This page is starred and earmarked, in case you're wondering, and though I've lost my hold on the message these past few weeks, I'm trying to turn back to it. To "repent," maybe, in the truest sense of the word's etymology. Faith really is a practice.

    I had to Google "supersessionism" when I read your letter, so thank you for introducing me to a new idea. I haven't spent much time with it so I doubt I have much of value to offer, but I don't see how it fits here. As far as I can tell, BibleProject speaks of continuation, not replacement: the Bible is one unified story, pointing to Christ. This is one of those rare instances when I'm grateful for my fresh biblical mind, uncluttered by narratives and agendas forced down my throat at a tender age. Instead, I have cluttered it with ideas, theories, and arguments sought out of my own volition. I am desperate for guidance, but I get to filter it through a fully developed, adult mind—*my* mind. Granted, your affront at my initial (highly emotional, it bears repeating) interpretation of violence sent me on an obsessive odyssey of education, and my beliefs have evolved quite a bit, but to me it's still plain as day that God's judgment can manifest in mortal consequences. I feel embarrassed and not a little ashamed that I blamed God for human violence, and childish in my failure to see the consistency of his character over time. Yet, I arrived at those problematic conclusions on my own, with all the freedom in the world to err and doubt my way into a kind of understanding. You challenged me, but I got to choose what to do with

---

1. Nouwen, *Inner Voice of Love*, 13.

that pushback. Starting from scratch doesn't make my interpretations more accurate—I'm sure they're less credible for their newness—but it gives me breathing room.

Speaking of digression! Back to supersessionism. I just don't understand how we could possibly read the Old and New Testaments as anything *but* a "unified story that points to Jesus," as the BibleProject claims. If Jesus isn't the fulfillment of the promises of the Old Testament, then he loses the credibility of thousands of years of prophecy. I'm writing and deleting, writing and deleting, because I'm floundering to even understand how we're meant to read the texts, if not as a continuous thread. The same God reigns, slow to anger and relentlessly forgiving, if sometimes harsh (I would argue necessarily so) in his judgment. His forgiving spirit doesn't emerge with Jesus—it's almost unfathomable how patient he is with his chosen people in the Old Testament. The psalms are riddled with forgiveness, but this passage in Isaiah is one of my current favorites: "Though your sins are like scarlet, they shall be as white as snow; though they are red as crimson, they shall be like wool" (Isa 1:18 NIV). The one thing we can count on in the Old Testament is that God's people will screw up. In fact, most of the time they're screwing up, and they suffer retribution but not true abandonment. God always comes back. That same promise of judgment shows up in the New Testament as well, and from the mouth of superhumanly sinless and loving Jesus, no less: "Not everyone who says to me, 'Lord, Lord,' will enter the kingdom of heaven, but only he who does the will of my Father who is in heaven. Many will say to me on that day, 'Lord, Lord, did we not prophesy in your name, and in your name drive out demons and perform many miracles?' Then I will tell them plainly, 'I never knew you. Away from me, you evildoers!'" (Matt 7:21–23 NIV). But then, crucifixion. For all of us.

The point I'm clumsily trying to make is that for me, the Bible is not a miniseries but an epic; it's one book with one story and one God. Of course Jewish readers won't read the Hebrew Bible with a Christian lens, and of course I will, right? We belong to different traditions, each of us choosing to believe the story we believe in. Christian readers *should* understand the Hebrew Bible in its Jewish context, not only because that's the accurate lens, but because Jesus came from that tradition. We have to know the Old Testament to know Jesus, but we can also understand it as always pointing to Christ, because it was always pointing to *someone*. For Christians, that's Christ. For Jews, it's not.

That said, I understand the implications of a supersessionist belief that Christians replace the Jews as God's chosen people. Only think of the atrocities committed (falsely) in the name of Christ against people who don't follow him. It's not my business to decide or even to know who will be saved, but rather to live like Christ and hope for the best. Bauerschmidt writes poignantly about this in *The Love That Is God*, when he asks and answers, "How might it be the case that loss of life in the kingdom is a real possibility, and yet God's universal will for human salvation is not thwarted? . . . The question of who will be saved is one case where a certain reverent agnosticism, a willingness not to know, commands itself."[2] We don't need to disown or condemn the Jews, or anyone else for that matter, to glorify the Christian God. I also think that as long as we don't wield our conviction like a hammer, it's okay that we think our story is "right." If we didn't, the binding of religion would unravel completely and we'd be left with vague spirituality (shudder).

That leads me to address your experience of not always seeing Scripture as authoritative, but briefly, because this letter is turning into its own epic. If Scripture isn't authoritative, divinely inspired, then the hard lines of Christianity dissolve, and we have a whole different thing. This doesn't mean we take each word of the Bible literally—if we did that with the parables we'd all be running around cursing fig trees—but that we thoughtfully apply context, notice evolution in the text, and imagine what Jesus might say about today's society had he been born into modernity instead of the ancient world.

Today you lamented in a text that your previous letter didn't directly respond to the threads in mine, so I'll insert this declaration in black and white to keep us both accountable: next time, we write about hope.

Love,
Devon

---

2. Bauerschmidt, *Love That Is God*, 113.

JULY 14, 2022

Dear Katherine,

 I can't tell yet if this will be about hope, but I needed to write another letter. It's been a strange couple of weeks with this job transition, and with the crushing weight of truth about a situation I won't write about here, and I've spent a good deal of my free time buried in Scripture, theology, and prayer. It's one of those moments when I'm clinging to faith, hoping that the tiny muscles in my fingers can hold on tight enough to weather this most recent storm, but I'm not quite sure what "weathering" means here. As I wrote that, it occurred to me that I'm seeing this like an acute episode of distress, that once endured will come to an end and then fade away, leaving no consequence or evidence of its presence. What foolishness. When has it ever worked that way?

 I started this letter because I've been turning over in my head BibleProject's explanation of God's judgment. I feel like the over-eager child-scholar I was, waving her hand around in class, near-to-bursting with desire to give the right answer. "Knowing" gave me worth, and others knowing I knew made me delirious with pride. Insecurity makes even children vulnerable to sin, and the same insecurity compels my adult self to wave my hand around now, blurting out an answer to a question no one asked, to let you know I've learned something since my original fumble with God's violence. I've been reading and listening and reflecting and I'm smarter now. I'm smart! I swear!

 It strikes me in this moment that I may also be the driving force of digression in our exchanges, but oh well.

 Anyway. I've been listening to the BibleProject's *Character of God* series and it's bringing it all together for me. They spend a long time on God's anger—or more accurately his judgment, which he frequently enacts out of sorrow—and how it reaches the people of the world. In their episode about the flood, they get around to the conclusion that God doesn't unleash anything on humanity that we haven't begged for through our own sinful actions. By withdrawing order from the world, he's not punishing us so much as abandoning us to, and hastening along, the natural consequences of our actions. Humans want to ravage the natural world by violence? "Okay," God laments, "I'll hurry that along for you." And then, he starts again. He starts again with a covenant never to subject humanity to the same fate, and he's stayed in relationship since.

To me, this is tremendous and changes the whole game. I almost can't believe I needed it explained so bluntly, because this bears out in Scripture again and again. Natural consequences. How could I have missed that? God does not punish in anger; he leaves us to our own devices. Humanity is utterly broken and fated to sin, but he loves us so violently that he would impose order on the known universe so that we might flourish. It's incredible that this happens even in moments. How beloved are we.

I guess I wrote about hope after all.

With gratitude to BibleProject, and to you,
Devon

July 18, 2022

Dear Devon,

 One of the things I love—and perhaps fear—about this project is that it is unfolding in real time. We did not craft a tidy outline. There is no map. There are only responses, a back-and-forth of ever-deepening relationship with one another and with God. There's a vulnerability to this that is beautiful and terrifying. There is no way to come off as cool or smart. Not unless we're going to redact our emotional reactions or edit out our rejected conclusions. If we are truly open to one another and open to the refining fire of God's Spirit, we are going to change. Maybe in some ways we welcome, but maybe also in some ways that feel like dying.

 Speaking of dying: the other day you let me listen to you sing in the chapel. The acoustics of that space are intense. The concrete surfaces aren't kind to consonants, but the stained glass windows and high ceiling amplify emotion. You sang a song by Jensen McRay with an echoing line so sharp and searing I could feel it in my bones: *my ego dies at the end*. Ego death is the thing we don't want; ego death is the thing we need. The song ended up lodged firmly in my ear all weekend. You've said you aren't much moved by songs that are about God—except, of course, for hymns in a church. But I can't hear that song and not hear all the theology flowing through it. My God, she sings of drowning in dreams and a baptism that burns! If it's a song about being human, it's a song about God. In the Eugene Peterson book I'm reading now, *Run with the Horses*, Peterson claims, "There are no religious types. There are only human beings, every one created for a relationship with God that is personal and eternal."[1] I guess there's a part of me that doesn't believe there is such a thing as a song that isn't about God. And that song about the death of an ego, especially sung by your beautiful voice in that sacred place, sounded like a prayer. Personal and eternal.

 Ultimately I think that's why I do love songs that are explicitly about God. They give me words to pray when prayer so often eludes me. I envy your ability to pray. I am good at praying professionally—I can write pretty words that cover all the proverbial bases. I can even unspool a reasonably eloquent extemporaneous prayer on behalf of a group of people. You've heard me do that a few times in the Seim room at church, at the conclusion of the Moms in Faith meeting and to close the trauma processing group you

---

1. Peterson, *Run with the Horses*, 133.

led. But I still struggle, after all these years, to pray alone. Maybe that's not the right way to put it; there's no such thing as praying alone, because God is purportedly with us. But you know what I mean.

In a journal I kept in seminary, I reflected on my failure to pray with equal parts sorrow and acceptance. *I do not pray*, my confession began. *I don't know how to pray. I don't like to close my eyes, clasp my hands, and start talking in my head toward God. Of course, I know that isn't my only option. I know that I could sit in silence, or read from a prayer book, or ride my bicycle down the street blessing everything I see. I don't do any of that stuff, either. Even when I am desperate, rarely do I mention anything to God. God and I are not on speaking terms. I'm like the quirky, solitary, yet totally productive worker in the cubicle on the third floor. Never actually talks to the boss, and the boss seldom thinks about him except to vaguely acknowledge gratitude that the worker is such a company man. I want to do the work of God on earth, to be part of the saints marching in—there just isn't much for us to talk about in the meantime. I like to be in church surrounded by people who know how to pray. But I do not know how to do it myself.*

A lot has changed since I scribbled these words in my journal. One time, when I was an especially desperate first-year pastor, my first authentic prayer in decades bubbled up in my gut and rumbled under my breath: *God, help me get my shit together.* I marveled at the profundity of my profanity. I really meant that prayer in a way I'd hadn't meant a prayer since I was a child, repeatedly begging Jesus to come into my heart. (Have I told you about that yet?) Nothing ever happened after those childhood petitions. I remained hamstrung by shame and angst. In retrospect, I think God did fulfill my later request. I did get my shit together, more or less, enough to get back to my work as a company man. But prayer remains an uneasy practice for me. It does not come naturally to me. I still can't say that I have learned how to pray. I am learning how to pray.

I get tangled up in the questions. Do we pray because it "works"? Do we pray because it makes us feel better? What does it mean to say that a prayer has been "answered"?

Prayer, and how it is answered—or unanswered, as the case may be—is incredibly tough to think through, because it isn't merely an exercise in theory. It's a matter of life and death, sickness and health, liberation and bondage. And it's so very personal. Christians are supposed to pray about the stuff that matters most: for loved ones who are sick, for reconciliation between husbands and wives and parents and children, for traveling mercies when our friends and family members board planes and take off in cars. Christians are supposed to pray for the oppressed and downtrodden, the hungry and the poor. My carefully crafted, heartfelt-yet-curated public prayers are full of such appeals.

I am quick to tell my parishioners that the ambiguous nature of prayer does not mean we worship a capricious God who sometimes cares and sometimes doesn't. The deepest, most foundational beliefs of the Christian tradition insist that God is loving and merciful and worthy of our trust. (And just. God is just, and that BibleProject series about the *Character of God* is next after I finish the one on the *Tree of Life*.) We are well aware that God doesn't protect us from suffering, but he does love us enough to suffer with us. I tell them we aren't ever going to understand why it seems like God answers one prayer and not another. I've been known to quote C. S. Lewis. (At least, I think it's a real C. S. Lewis quote. I think his character says it in *Shadowlands*, the movie about losing his wife, Joy.) "I pray because I can't help myself. I pray because I'm helpless. I pray because the need flows out of me all the time—waking and sleeping. It doesn't change God—it changes me."[2]

I like this: It doesn't change God, it changes me. And yet, there's this kernel of question in my heart, pondering if this is merely a hedge against the possibility that God isn't listening—that God is . . . not.

This is how that old journal entry ended: *Maj told me this summer that I had to pray, that nothing would ever make sense unless I pray. He was surprised when I confessed that I do not pray. I said that I have always felt as though I am walking around the perimeter of the place where God is, peering in the windows and feeling forsaken. Have I ever knocked on the arched front doors, or tried to turn the silver doorknob? Maj said the door would be insignificant if I just prayed. The walls themselves would dissolve.*

We are supposed to be writing about hope, and therein lies mine: I not only believe this is true. In the last few months—really, since I took that Plan B sabbatical that pulled me back from the brink of spiritual desolation and vocational burnout—I have started to notice that the edges of the walls are fading. I prayed through 150 psalms, albeit badly, mind wandering. If you can believe it, I'm *still* parked on Psalm 1. I've memorized it and can't stop hoping—can't stop praying?—that I'm going to be like a tree planted by streams of water, which bears fruit in its season.

---

2. See https://www.goodreads.com/quotes/1005539.

In *Run with the Horses*, Peterson quotes G. K. Chesterton: "As long as matters are really hopeful, hope is mere flattery or platitude. It is only when everything is hopeless that hope begins to be a strength at all. Like all the Christian virtues, it is as unreasonable as it is indispensable."[3] The sentiment reminds me of what you gleaned from Ellul. You said he defines "hope as the thing we hold on to when we have no reason to hope," and that this paradox gave you something to grasp onto. This is the only kind of hope that makes any sense to me. I can barely tolerate optimism. I hate it when people pretend everything is going to be okay (even though, to be clear, I desperately want everything to be okay). I crave the kind of honesty that names hope as unreasonable—perhaps even mere delusion. It's the same paradox that makes me distrust certainty. I can't stand when people equate faith and certainty any more than when they equate hope with optimism. I guess that is why I can live with the horrible possibility that God is not God—because it is within that very tremble of hopelessness, that admission of possible delusion, that my hope in the God who is God emerges.

There is more to say, but now I'm going to go pray, and hope some more of that wall comes tumbling down.

Love,
Katherine
    P.S. I still have that song in my head. Thank you.

---

3. Peterson, *Run with the Horses*, 168.

July 18, 2022

Dear Katherine,

    I have no business responding to your exquisite letter in the state I now find myself bone tired from dream-riddled sleep and thick with the lethargy of unhealthy coping behaviors—but if I only wrote after a good night of sleep then we wouldn't have much of a book on our hands. Your letter was mellifluous. I knew the feeling of the adjective I wanted to use before I found the word, because I felt carried along by your words. I know you've prayed about prayer because you've told me, but also because of how intimately acquainted you seem with every word in that section of your letter. I know it was meant to be funny, but the journal entry made me sad. This poor young woman, entering the priesthood, and the most accurate simile for her relationship with God is an indifferent office manager and his voiceless employee, ignored but diligently working . . . on what, exactly? I imagine, "the work of God on earth," but with what kind of motivation, God being so silent at the time?

    I am glad you are learning how to pray, though I am not sure what kind of achievement would elevate one from student to master. I had forgotten until your letter that one night after Bible study, I drove home and read the entirety of Nouwen's *With Open Hands*, but didn't pick it up again until right now. He says that prayer "demands a relationship in which you allow someone other than yourself to enter into the very center of your person, to see there what you would rather leave in darkness, and to touch there what you would rather leave untouched."[1] Doesn't that have a terrifying ring to it?! Prayer is exposing our soft underbellies and twisted insides, and "by putting on a semblance of beauty, by holding back everything dirty and spoiled,"[2] we betray our fears. Our fears that God isn't listening; that he can't or won't save us; that we'll have to make sense of an unanswered prayer; that God isn't the giver of good things; or that God is . . . not, as your anxiety questions. When we fear we offer prayers of little faith: "Carefully reckoned, even stingy, and . . . upset by every risk. There is no danger of despair and no chance for hope. We become midgets in a world of tiny things."[3] For Nouwen, and for me, prayer means laying bare our whole selves. And by

---

1. Nouwen, *With Open Hands*, 19.
2. Nouwen, *With Open Hands*, 25.
3. Nouwen, *With Open Hands*, 71.

the way, he is on board with prayers of petition and for concrete things because of the authenticity inherent in the request. He says that asking for something concrete is letting God into the nitty-gritty of our everyday lives and expressing unlimited trust. I love Nouwen so much for being like, "It's all okay! Just trust, hope, and it's all okay."

Did you catch it above, the implication that we must risk despair? He ups the ante and says, "Despair is possible only for someone who knows what it means to hope,"[4] and this both settles my heart and breaks it because I knew it. I *knew* that the despair enshrouding me after this weekend is because of that dangerous little bit of hope I walked away with, and if Nouwen's right, the former is here to stay as long as the latter lingers. He's right, though. Sometimes when I'm overwhelmed, my body does a cruel trick where it disconnects me from my emotions, as neat as if it flicked a switch, and plunges me into apathy. Usually this happens during times of unbearable sadness, and it saves me from my pain but it also keeps me from God. When I'm like that I'm afraid of hope, and God is hope. The kind of hope that insists upon the possibility of good when all the evidence is to the contrary. That kind of hope hurts so much it feels physical. It hurts so deeply that it saps the strength needed to fend off despair. That's the kind of hope I got a taste of. Being with Ian this weekend felt so right that I dared to hope for a different future, and I do not know if I can survive that feeling. I believe God wants only good for me, but I'm not naive enough to believe that I understand his will, or that his "good" won't look a thing like what I hope for. That's the key, though—"when we live with hope we do not get tangled up with concerns for how our wishes will be fulfilled."[5] Hope can't be so narrow, and it's not for me—what I hope is for peace and restoration, whether or not that comes with health for him and stability for me—but therein lies the threat of despair.

Last night I prayed not in hope, but in anger. I'm uneasy about my anger toward God, but I suppose it's better than indifference. This precious relationship of mine, the one that inspires the hope and despair of preceding paragraphs, is so full of holes and heartache from injuries incurred over the course of decades. I'm angry that they ever happened and I don't understand, so I stormed over to my grotto and prayed up a petulant little storm. I stared down that cold, white Virgin Mary, presiding over my own little Gethsemane, and asked my questions over and over: *How could you?*

---

4. Nouwen, *With Open Hands*, 71.
5. Nouwen, *With Open Hands*, 73.

Why? What kind of cruel God would lead us here? I'm sure it was an entertaining spectacle in God's eyes, this mortal woman shaking her tiny fists at The Creator and demanding an answer she wouldn't understand anyway.

I did calm down, though, and in the sheer silence I remembered what I felt driving away Saturday afternoon. The avalanche of sadness, fury, and fear had all but obliterated it from my memory, but a part of me recalled an overpowering love. After an intense night of weepy conversations, I left feeling beloved. By him, but also by the God who is between us. Kierkegaard says that God needs to be the "middle term" in a relationship, which means, "To help another human being to love God is to love another man; to be helped by another human being to love God is to be loved,"[6] and that is a hallmark of our relationship. Amidst pain and longing and tidal waves of despair is the presence of God. We are bereft of certainty, but within the context of that relationship, I feel closer to God.

All sorts of negative emotions are threatening to spill out over the hope like a legion, so I will force myself to stop there. I don't feel it, so all the more reason to protect that nuisance, hope.

Love,
Devon

---

6. Kierkegaard, *Works of Love*, 112.

JULY 29, 2022

Dear Devon,

  I audibly gasped when I read the last line of your letter. I've never thought of hope as a nuisance. I've thought of it as an asset, albeit one that is often beyond reach. But you're right—hope can be a nuisance. Even a menace. But we protect it anyway, knowing we need it.

  You are reminding me I need to read more Nouwen. I've lost track of how many people have told me I should read *Life of the Beloved*, especially after I had the word "beloved" tattooed on my left wrist. I've only read *Love, Henri*—his letters to various personal and professional correspondents. One of the books on my to-read list is his *Letters to Marc About Jesus*, as I sometimes think of this project as my *Letters to Devon About Jesus*. Today over breakfast we talked about vulnerability (again), and writing (again). So much of what can be said about those things can also be said about prayer, at least the way Nouwen talks about prayer. Here we are, granting one another access to our soul's interiors. Soft underbellies exposed like the complicated animals we are. I know I am addressing this to you, each epistle beginning with those simple, vintage words: *Dear Devon*. But it's striking to me that you called this project Love Letters to *God*. I would like to believe that this gloriously unwieldy project is about friendship, mutual ministry, and intellectual inquiry—but that it is also a practice of prayer in community. I mean, I think about your experience entering the confessional to disencumber yourself from sin and shame, and my experience of taking on the mantle of priest extending God's own mercy and forgiveness. What is this but prayer?

  It astonishes me how much human relationships can take us into the presence of God. I know things remain bewildering and complicated with Ian, and that the pendulum might have swung back to something more like acquiescence, if not despair. But it doesn't change that it's still the relationship that ushered you into faith, and that still lifts you into Holy Presence.

  This morning as we circled back to vulnerability and boundaries and what parts of our stories and our selves we weave into these pages, I admitted I have some inhibitions. A lot of it is being a mother of two human beings I recognize are distinctly separate from me. Their shit is not my shit; their hearts are not my heart. There is so much I could write about what it is to parent my children, but I can't. I will continue to tell you those stories and ask those questions in the privacy of café tables.

But there's so much more buttressing my boundaries. I published my first memoir at age thirty-two. I'll never forget when I was on my way to a writing workshop to work on my manuscript, I picked up an *Oprah Magazine*. There was an article encouraging readers to "hold as self-evident your right to ignore memoirs by people who have barely cracked their 30s." I took this stupidly hard, and for years felt defensive about having been a part of the generational trend toward narrative nakedness, and anxious that I didn't have anything worth saying. And then I published another memoir at age thirty-six, and that's when things really started to feel messy. I wrote about a marriage as it was still happening. We were still fumbling, very imperfectly, toward wisdom and grace. We got ourselves tangled up in the worst argument the day the book boxes arrived, and I felt like a hypocritical jackass. And then just having all of that stuff out there. My life was no longer mine to tend, but *material*. Material that can be reviewed on freaking *Amazon*. No matter that a lot of people said very nice things. "M. Glass" gave it one star and said this: "It is troubling to me that this is as published as a book rather than a journal for good therapy work. There are a lot of other people's lives on the pages of this book. I hope for the best for them all, and hope the next chapter doesn't get turned into another book for public consumption rather than private amends."[1] Yeah, M. It is troubling to me, too. But also: screw you! I wasn't merely burned by the experience of publishing personal material. I was scorched.

There is another layer, too.

Shortly after I signed a contract to write *Very Married*, a friend and fellow Christian author warned me about spiritual warfare. In her experience, when she wrote about an aspect of her life, it became vulnerable to attack. When she'd written about parenting, for example, she felt as though her relationships with her kids sustained deep wounds—as though some sinister force invaded with chaos and sabotage. She meant well when she told me this. She knew I was setting out to write about my marriage, and she wanted me to be alert for signs of marital distress. When my marriage did suffer in the wake of my little book, I deliberated incessantly on the possibility that some iniquitous spirit might have been to blame.

---

1. M. Glass, Review of *Very Married: Field Notes on Love and Fidelity*, by Katherine Willis Pershey, Amazon, Dec. 19, 2016, https://www.amazon.com/product-reviews/1513800175.

Liberal mainline Christianity places precious little faith in spiritual warfare. It's not even that we actively disbelieve in it. It doesn't even come up. Our theological imaginary is far too sophisticated for demons and devils. Sometimes I fret that the liberal mainline imaginary might also be too sophisticated for angels and—God forbid—God.

Before we hatched our plan to write letters to one another, I was going to write a more traditional doctoral thesis about the obstacles to faith in the secular age. I was terrified doing so would invite the same sort of spiritual warfare waged against my marriage. (No matter that my marriage survived, stronger than before. The battles were brutal.) I desperately long to know God and to experience God's presence in a world seemingly leached of holiness. If I committed this yearning for faithfulness to the page, I was convinced I would bid the demons of doubt to assault me. I would make myself an easy target for Screwtape and his compatriots.

Last summer, I sheepishly confessed some of these fears to a friend. She clearly did not know what to make of my confession; I suspect she thought I was being ridiculous. But that same night I had a vivid dream. It was a nightmare without a plot. I was not chased by monsters or undressed before a crowd. Rather, I was filled with dread and terror in the presence of something palpable but intangible. Pure evil. I have rarely encountered such fathomless fear in my waking hours. It was how I imagine I would feel if a man held a blade to my throat, a totalizing physiological reality that leaves no room for breath. I was frantic, but in my sleepy state, I was pinned to the bed, paralyzed by fright. And then I heard something—something tangible. An inscrutable disturbance on the first floor, followed by Betsy's paws clicking on the hardwood floor. It was loud enough to wake me up. In the morning I discovered a framed art print tucked between the decorative pillows; the mystery sound that dragged me into consciousness was the picture toppling from its nail and startling the sleeping dog.

I can still conjure the sensation of being in the shadow of this dream-state evil. I remain unsettled by the thought of a demonic force entering my house and/or subconscious. But a year or so later, I find it all a bit funny. At the time, it was galling to me that the very object of my deepest desire—an unmistakable encounter with the Holy Presence—remained largely elusive, whereas I was apparently experiencing the Unholy Presence. I wanted to know the Triune God, not the ornery devil.

There I was, longing for God in a secular age. I know there was a part of me that welcomed a whiff of spiritual warfare. Spiritual warfare is marvelously unsecular. And after all, confrontations with evil spirits corroborate the existence of good ones, don't they? But the Holy Spirit wins, as she did in that midnight skirmish. I can no longer accept the explanations of my secular mind. The adhesive on the Velcro strips I'd used to fasten the hand-drawn map of Ohio to the wall had not failed. An angel of the Lord popped that picture from its place on the wall.

At breakfast we talked about superstitions. You cringe when I acknowledge out loud that I still haven't contracted Covid; I shudder to see a hat casually tossed onto a bed. I have some lingering superstitions about writing and warfare, but they've faded a bit. Especially since we embarked on these letters. My faith has not been assailed; it has been strengthened. I have had more poignant encounters with Holy Presence this past year than the forty-one years prior—or rather, I've noticed and named these encounters as such. God may well have been just as active and present but I did not have the eyes to see or the ears to hear.

You'll be happy to know I have been praying more. I'm not the company man toiling away anonymously in the third-floor cubicle anymore. Praise God from whom all blessings flow.

Love,
Katherine

August 10, 2022

Dear Katherine,

This is my fourth attempt at responding to your letter. I have been struggling to write for weeks, and—I probably exhaust this expression with overuse, but I always mean it—it's starting to break my heart. I know where the words went. They are trapped, along with whatever good I have in me, in a spiral of spiritual warfare. Losing the ability to write seems a natural consequence of losing my grip on the commandments; it's hard to write about Christ when I'm floundering to live like him. I know I'm only as weak as the next human, utterly depraved and built to sin, but not all spiritual warfare ends in victory and that petrifies me. I usually feel bashful asking for prayers, but I probably need them right now.

I dabble in superstition, but spiritual warfare isn't something that befalls me or catches me unaware. I am perfectly capable of getting in my own way, thank you very much, and the only thing rendering me vulnerable to attack is me. It's not that I lose the eyes to see or the ears to hear during these battles, but rather that I blind my eyes and stop up my ears. A spiritual director commented that addicts who seek out a substance are really seeking God, but that isn't true for me. When I abuse my "substances" of choice, it's more like I know exactly where to find God, and then I run headlong in the opposite direction. It's a kind of madness to willfully cast off God's love. It's a terminally ill patient rejecting the curative miracle drug, and on the surface it's incomprehensibly irrational. From a psychological perspective though, it makes all the sense in the world; some of us cannot bear to be seen in our shame. It's too dangerous to the Self. God's love for us has nothing to do with our worthiness, but at times I feel so undeserving that I actively spurn him. It's a terribly conflicted experience of intentionality independent from desire; I am conscious of my sins, but I hate them as I commit them. It was Ian who equated it to self-immolation, and he's right that it's like setting fire to my soul. It's also like playing God, doling out justice in his place, and it's blasphemy.

All that to say, I don't share your concern that these letters will invite spiritual warfare. To the contrary, everything I know about God suggests that the laying bare of our souls will fling the divine floodgates wide open. He wants us to invite him in. At the time of *Very Married*'s publication, there were unresolved marital issues that the book implied had been figured out, and artifice beckons, "Test me." As you are wont to remind me, Jesus never condemns a contrite sinner, because it's not our transgressions God can't tolerate, but our defiance in repenting of them. Tying up a mess in a tidy little bow is a denial of our need for God's intervention. It's like, "Move along, God! Nothing to see here! We have it all under control!" That charade isn't exactly on par with my mad sprints, described above, but it is a form of apostasy that I don't think we are guilty of in these letters.

In fact, one of my great insecurities about this project is how authentic I have been in my developing scriptural interpretation. It is painfully obvious that I'm learning in real time. Even if I wanted to tie up the messiness with a bow, there isn't a ribbon to be found. Do you know how embarrassed I am about my harebrained "God modeled violence to humans" theory? Probably, since I've mentioned it a dozen times since. I am deep in the prophets, and nothing could be more clear to me now than God's repudiation of bloodshed. Even David, chosen by God, was unfit to build the temple because of the blood on his hands. Ellul writes about violence as a detestable necessity to state building, not to be defended but likely to be engaged in. He's insistent that Christians must turn from violence if they are to live like Christ, but accurate in his observation that many of us try to justify why we don't ("righteous" revolutions, for instance). To those people he says, "The important thing is that, when he uses violence, the Christian knows very well that he is doing wrong, sinning against the God of love, and . . . is increasing the world's disorder."[1] Whenever it's committed, no matter if it feels absolutely necessary, violence is never condoned. Anyway the point is that between Ellul, Heschel, Scripture, and the BibleProject, I've developed a radically different understanding of God's character, and total strangers will get a front seat to every stumbling step of that journey. I hate that everyone will know my intellectual and spiritual shortcomings. It kills me that even if I want to later, I can't edit them out and break the continuity of correspondence. If I'm lucky, maybe God will notice and see fit to correct them. "Blessed is the man whom thou chastenest, O Lord" (Ps 93:12a KJV). In my first draft of this letter, composed nearly a week ago, I wrote pretty obnoxiously about my fear that readers would attack my intellect. I say obnoxiously, because in hindsight I can see it's a superficial concern, a vanity of vanities. However, each scrapped draft and false start of this letter made it abundantly clear that my intellect can survive detractors, but my personal life could take a hit. As it is, Ian asked me to use a pseudonym,

---

1. Ellul, *Violence*, 137.

and by the time anyone reads this he will be anonymized out of my story with a different name. Part of the pain of the last several weeks has to do with him, and I've been doing literary gymnastics trying to resolve the tension between needing to write about it and wanting to protect not only his privacy, but ours together. He's too wrapped up in my personal and spiritual life to extricate him from these letters, and if the conclusion of this project finds me explicitly and not only technically single, how then will I feel about his name (well, not his name but his presence) littering these pages? Heartbroken or not, I'll have to deal with his indelible presence in my public-facing identity. And what if he reads that sentence, and it breaks his heart with its faithlessness? I don't really know what to do here, Katherine, and don't even get me started on the paralysis of whether to write about my parents. It was an illuminating weekend, with a long-suspected but never confirmed family secret making its way to the surface, and undoubtedly I have many therapy sessions ahead of me to reconcile with it. It's not that I need the world to know about that trauma, but that it's inextricably tied up in my relationship with faith and sacrament, judgment and forgiveness. In a powerful way, the story of the secret is mine to reckon with and to share if I see fit, but it doesn't belong to me exclusively. Could I choose to leave it out and leapfrog over it to a safer, more scholarly reflection? Yes. Is it selfish to write about it? Maybe, but not necessarily. I just don't know, Katherine. When I read *Very Married*, we were mere weeks into our fledgling relationship, and the startling vulnerability of your writing accelerated our intimacy. You carried it off with such literary aplomb, and your boldness enraptured me even as it struck me that you were certifiably insane. Who *does* that? What kind of maniac exposes her soft underbelly to a harsh world, and then hands over a razor with which to slash it open with greater convenience? My own vulnerability feels irrepressible, not at all a product of comfort with discomfort, but the author of *Very Married* wrote unapologetically. As I tore through one poignant, funny, beautifully crafted chapter after the next, my terror for her mounted. Please understand this is not an indictment on the quality of your writing. To the contrary, it was the success of it that made it susceptible to censure; we tear down what threatens us. I desperately admired your courage, but I knew I could never be so brave. And now here I am, another lunatic readying herself for the slaughter.

  Are we crazy for doing this? Honestly, maybe. Speaking only for myself, publishing this would be opening up myself and others to a world of hurt. I also know I will feel more sorrow if these pages never see the light of day, so it looks like it's onward for me.

Godspeed to us both,
Devon

P.S. I want to tell you about my dream. It was plotless and might therefore make for a dull story, but it was also a transcendent experience. Heschel writes about "prophetic sympathy," a term I hadn't yet heard but immediately fell in love with, and describes it as "the assimilation of the prophet's emotional life to the divine."[2] I am no prophet, but what happened in that dream felt something like that. I swear, I felt God's feelings.

The backstory of the dream is my recent obsession with understanding the "hidden bond between the word of wrath and the word compassion, between 'consuming fire' and 'everlasting love.'"[3] I couldn't make sense of that relationship, perhaps because of my childhood unfamiliarity with rules and consequences. Of the former we had few, and in regards to the latter I could usually talk my way out of them. I sympathize with my parents, raising two strikingly different children in separate households, but there wasn't enough structure for me to come away with a healthy fear of consequences for my actions, or even an ingrained belief that I would suffer any. Even as an adult I managed to dodge the fallout from my innumerable errors, often through deception, so it wasn't until several years ago and a transgression that wouldn't stay hidden that I truly grasped the gravity of my choices. I have come to judgment late, with fear and trembling.

Back to the dream. I went to bed after watching *Tree of Life* for the first time, and I don't know how Terrence Malick got it past the secular academy, because that is a decidedly Christian film. It illuminates the "hidden bond" of my obsession, and it must have been kicking around my brain when I fell asleep. How do I describe this dream that was all embodied energy (says the somatic therapist)? What I felt was this: First, one side of my body blossomed with this warm, golden, radiant light. I felt it on every inch of skin and in each organ and nerve ending; I could feel and see myself glowing. I knew this energy was God's love. I just knew it. Then, the other side of my body was flooded with a heavier, somehow more piercing light. It was passion free of pain, menacing but not injurious, and again it wound itself through my whole system and poured out of me. Finally, my whole

2. Heschel, *Prophets*, 31.
3. Heschel, *Prophets*, 29.

body became a vessel. My feet left the ground and the energy that could only have been God's held me suspended in the air. I pulsed with light and love, retribution and forgiveness, and as I hung there I knew—I *knew*—they were all the same. God allows us to endure the natural consequences of our actions out of pure love. If he didn't, humans would be extinct by now. I'm not saying they're fun, and I still fear he has more in store for me, but I've felt the refining fire in my blood and in my bones and I am grateful. Okay, now I'm really done.

Love once more,
Devon

August 27, 2022

Dear Katherine,

    I was going to add to our apocryphal file, but then I had an experience that felt important to write about here. I know I'm out of turn again—I'm also writing this at Solemn Oath with *the* most delightful hazy IPA, and it's entirely possible my skills go the way of that delicious beer at some point in this letter—so who knows where this letter will land in the catalog, but we can sort that out later.

    This morning, I started to respond to your letter with a deluge of anxieties and an abundance of anger, but something about it felt wrong. I had self-pity for breakfast and was sick with it all day, and something about that felt wrong too. It's not that I was totally out of line in feeling it, but that self-pity really isn't my speed. It evokes a kind of disgust in me because I am so impossibly fortunate, but it got its hooks in me this weekend. It has not been a good week in some respects. For weeks I've been avoiding confronting potentially damning questions, but on Tuesday I opened the emotional floodgates and let it all wash over me. I can't believe I didn't drown, because the intensity of it nearly swept me away. I *didn't* drown, and that's important to recognize, but I spent the subsequent days trying to ride the waves of truth that keep surging up. I got answers I never wanted, but I don't want to go into that because that's not the point of this letter. The point is what I did with that deluge of anxieties, that abundance of anger.

    I've written to you about my sun salutation practice, but I'm not sure if I explained that I use it as prayer—a moving meditation, as my yoga guru Erin Sampson would say. When I lose myself to my emotions, I do sets of thirty-six sun salutations to connect to God and to love. The God that is love, the love that is God. I needed that today, but nine salutes in I found myself embroiled with anger. I had forgotten about love and it turns out that that feels terrible, no matter how valid my anger. Kierkegaard writes that "love abides," and he illustrates it with an anecdote about a rupture in a relationship. One person breaks it off and says as much, but the lover (the "lover" for Kierkegaard is the fictional, literary device of a person who loves as Christ does) "abides." The lover says, "All is not over between us; we are still midway in the sentence; it is only the sentence which is not complete."[1] This is unreal to me. We keep loving through time and distance?

---

1. Kierkegaard, *Works of Love*, 284.

We keep loving even when discouraged from doing so? Did you know that Kierkegaard never married the woman he loved, Regine? I think he probably should have and he suffered for that, but I digress again. I thought about love abiding as I roiled in anger on my mat, and I changed course. I started sending out love instead of anger, and immediately I felt at peace. Hand to God, I smiled as I planked, and I did that thirty-two more times because I was enjoying myself so much that thirty-six wasn't enough.

The situation that provoked such anger and sadness has not been resolved, and I fear the eventual resolution could be a painful one, but what I don't feel any more is anger. I don't feel animosity toward another human being, and that is good. So, so mercifully good. Anger is useful. It tells us when something is not okay and it is not to be suppressed, but it's also meant to have a short life span. Holding onto it corrodes our insides and we suffer for that. Love doesn't banish anger, and it shouldn't, but it makes it a whole hell of a lot easier to bear. When it's present, anger can be the tool it's designed to be and not the nuclear bomb we so often construct out of it. It saved me today because it is a mandate of our faith, and not because I felt it easily. We must love, Katherine. We are commanded to love, and that commandment is the single most loving act of our God. What a blessing.

I love and cherish *you* so very much,
Devon

Interlude: A Text Conversation, September 9, 2022

Devon ✝:
>Dude, the book of Judith 🙌
>
>I read it all in one sitting because it was so compelling
>
>I also learned a new word: anthropopathy. It's fun to say.

Katherine:
>What does it mean??
>
>One of my kids is sick so I think Indy is off the table
>
>😭

Devon ✝:
>Nooooo
>
>oh my gosh I am so sorry
>
>It means ascribing passions and emotions to a nonhuman object, usually a deity

Katherine:
>It also just kind of sucks balls because now I just get to sit around not eating gluten and dairy (or beer)
>
>Alllll weekend

Devon ✝:
>I am laughing out loud because that really does sound abysmal

Katherine:
>Also when we first met you probably didn't imagine me sending you texts with the phrase "sucks balls"

Devon ✝:
>I certainly did not. I was trying to suss out if it was okay to swear around you.

Katherine:

I just met with a woman whose whole family is being baptized on Sunday night

Not night

I don't know where night came from

Sunday morning

Katherine:

I love baptisms, so much.

Devon ✝:

Baptisms are a beautiful thing.

I definitely wanna talk more about mine. I still want you to do it, but I don't wanna do it at First Congo. I think I would also like to invite the people from my small group, because I understand the importance of having people there and I think I want that now, but I don't know if I would feel comfortable doing that quite yet. Also I just think an immersion would be so cool

Katherine:

I am open. I would check in with Pastor Dan if there are stipulations around baptism in their tradition—I assume they are ecumenical about it, but I'd just make sure.

Devon ✝:

Hmm. I don't know if that would deter me.

But I guess I'll ask

That would bug me if they wouldn't let me be a member because a pastor from another denomination baptized me

Katherine:

I get that—but I highly value making a covenant commitment to be part of a local church and I would feel so badly if a rogue baptism complicated things for you

Devon ✝:

Yeah that would be a huge bummer. I'll ask him

Katherine:

I mean, for my own part, I have to get over my convictions around baptism happening in the context of communal worship—i.e., not privately

But I love you enough I can get over myself!

Devon †:
But I want it to be communal, just not in front of a whole congregation

I really do want to/plan to invite my small group

Could we do it in a chapel?

We can rent a dunk tank it'll be great

Katherine:
I get that—but, it's technically still private. Think of the way Bauerschmidt talks about the essence of the body of Christ. It's like, whoever the Spirit compels to show up. I was pretty firm about this before Covid—Rich would do private baptisms but I would not. With Covid it would have lacked pastoral integrity not to offer private baptisms, so now I've done plenty. But honestly, even as I'm typing this I am talking myself out of my rigidity. The Eunuch had a private baptism. Weddings are private, even though they are still Christian worship services (assuming they are, indeed, Christian weddings). Gravesides are private. So maybe it's more of a tradition thing than a theological thing that has me tied to this idea of Sunday morning worship being the place for baptisms.

Devon †:
Well you know I'm not fundamentally opposed to rigidity when it comes to doctrine, but I just don't understand the distinction between a community of choice in a community assembled at random

Picking up church is picking a community by choice

A church*

Katherine:
The whole "you don't choose who sits in the pew next to you" thing. Alan pushed back against it and thought it was one of Bauerschmidt's Catholicisms—because in the Catholic Church, you go to an assigned parish and you really are kind of stuck with the Christians in your neighborhood. Protestants changed that by giving people choice

(which, at its worst, makes a sort of religious market in which different "brands" of Christianity vie for "customers").

But I am not sure we "pick" a church so much as discern with the Spirit where we are called to go

Again, maybe this is me just pushing back against language that echoes late capitalism

Like, you pick a cantaloupe or a car; the Holy Spirit guides you to a community of faith

Did I anger you?

Devon †:

Oh my gosh not at all

I'm walking around. I guess even with that logic, which makes sense, I don't know if the community I'm guided to includes every stranger in the congregation. Like I did not pick you or my small group necessarily, but I ended up with you all through a series of choices I do actually feel like Providence because it all unfolded so fluently. I love Covenant and I think I will join that church, and I understand that joining at church means claiming that congregation, but I'm just not sure what is the offensive about involved in the community that I actually feel embedded in, personally

It definitely makes me want to do some research. Because I think about Jesus's baptism, it was him and a ton of strangers. So I understand how that could be a scriptural basis for that.

And it is important to me to do this the right way. The binding is important, as you know I love to say! It's just that I feel so uncomfortable standing up in front of a church and being on display like that

Katherine:

I get all of this. It's not offensive, at all. I wouldn't use that word. It's simply private. But private is not bad. Honestly, your reasoning for wanting a private baptism with your chosen community is so different from why many people ask for private baptisms. It's often coming from a place of purely cultural Christianity—like, they can't be bothered to be part of an actual worshiping community because they are doing this for the tradition and the photos and the cross-shaped cake from Kirschbaum's eaten in the fancy backyard soiree afterwards. I sound so judgy. But your reason for wanting a more curated gathering is more about gathering your soul friends, your true companions on your faith journey.

The teenagers who haven't been baptized and who need to be before they get confirmed definitely just feel uncomfortable standing up in front of church!

Devon ✝:
Oh my goodness no I don't want any of that

Katherine:
I know!!!

Devon ✝:
Maybe some booze though

Katherine:

I did read some articles by ultra conservative pastors poo-bah-ing private baptisms

I don't want to be legalistic

I just want to drench you in the waters of new life!!!

Devon ✝:

I would like everyone to drink together. Like Jesus did!

There's so much readinh I need to do

reading*

Katherine:

Same girl

And writing

I am frantically trying to get shit done because my day was once again not what it was supposed to be, thanks to the unexpected pediatrician visit

Devon ✝:

damn she's that sick?

Katherine:

Well, I thought it was strep and there's only one way to find out

September 3, 2022

Dear Devon,

I probably should have asked you before plopping that text thread into our Love Letters. I adore our steady stream of texts, and the unselfconscious way we chatter about bad days, brunch plans, relationships, theology, stuff we love, stuff we hate. I can't tell you how hard I laughed when you texted me from band practice, "Dude who likes this dazzling bouquet song and why are they making us sing it?" Because it was *me*, as I enlisted a GIF of Amy Poehler smugly pointing at herself to communicate. I am the one who loves that "horrible" song, and I cackled when you texted me after the church picnic lamenting that it had lodged itself in your head and was playing on repeat. Is it cruel to hope you get it in your head again now, Devon?

Maybe a small part of why I shared that thread is because I once again feel sheepish about my slow responses. I cannot believe it's been over a month. Maybe the text thread is my roundabout way of proving (to myself?) that I haven't been a terrible friend—that even though my life continues to be bananas with too many commitments in too many directions, our friendship perseveres and flourishes outside the context of these formal epistles. There are things I don't respond to here, because I have responded to them over lattes—sometimes even without words when words would only get in the way.

But I also shared it because I wanted to return to the topic of baptism. I did get anxious during our conversation yesterday, as I didn't want to offend you. With as chill as my tradition is about so many things (including, you know, *orthodoxy*), it is silly for me to be precious about whether or not your baptism happens in the context of a Sunday morning worship service, or in the company of soul friends. I know this. I really had to examine my reaction, and I do think it is less about traditional theological justifications and more about my nearly co-dependent relationship with the church as an institution. My relationship to the institutional church (via local congregations and denominational structures) has always been remarkably positive. I believed in the church when I did not believe in God. One of the only things I don't love about being a pastor is that I don't get to worship promiscuously. Have I ever told you what I used to do in college? I would go through these phases in which I could not get enough worship. I would go to Quaker meetings, and Episcopal Eucharists, and midweek Lutheran prayer services, and really awful contemporary services at a Vineyard church that met in a coffee shop. I love the random people who are thrown together, and the inherent challenge of being responsible for loving them. We've talked about reading something together, and I keep coming back to the *Screwtape Letters*. Take this quote:

> One of our great allies at present is the Church itself. Do not misunderstand me. I do not mean the Church as we see her spread but through all time and space and rooted in eternity, terrible as an army with banners. That, I confess, is a spectacle which makes our boldest tempters uneasy. But fortunately it is quite invisible to these humans. All your patient sees is the half-finished, sham Gothic erection on the new building estate. When he goes inside, he sees the local grocer with rather an oily expression on his face bustling up to offer him one shiny little book containing a liturgy which neither of them understands, and one shabby little book containing corrupt texts of a number of religious lyrics, mostly bad, and in very small print. When he gets to his pew and looks round him he sees just that selection of his neighbors whom he has hitherto avoided. You want to lean pretty heavily on those neighbors. Make his mind flit to and fro between an expression like "the body of Christ" and the actual faces in the next pew.[1]

I guess C. S. Lewis is with you on the bad religious lyrics.

To be clear, I am not doubling down. I'm letting up. As I exclaimed, I want to drench you in the waters of baptism. I want to trust that the Holy Spirit is going to lead us to the font (or dunk tank) when it is time, and you will say, "Look, here is water! What is to prevent me from being baptized?" And the Holy Spirit will whisper *nothing*, and I will baptize you in the name of the Father and of the Son and of the Holy Spirit. As I imagine this moment, Devon, I realize I too don't want it to be in front of a crowd. It's too intimate to baptize such an intimate friend on a public chancel. I am not your pastor any more than you are my therapist—and I can't even begin to tell you how much it means to me that you have invited me to be the one to render the sacrament. I am glad that you have Pastor Dan to be your pastor, and I hope you might even invite him to the occasion.

It strikes me that your plotless and transcendent dream was baptismal in nature. I won't lean into magical thinking about baptism, but I do hope that when you have received the sign and seal of the Holy Spirit, you will

---

1. Lewis, *Screwtape Letters*, 5–6.

have the capacity to fully surrender yourself to the grace and mercy of God. I want Romans 6:4–8 to be tattooed upon your consciousness in indelible ink.

It is now 5:56 p.m., and I told my children I would make dinner for them at 6:00 p.m. I was going to tell you all about the sermon I am planning to preach tomorrow—without notes! So I guess I have three minutes to sketch it out. As you know, I've memorized Psalm 1 and have been returning to it time and time again. I want to preach on that image of people as trees—that prayer to be made into a tree that is planted by streams of flowing water (*Look, there is water—again!*). The choice that is presented in this psalm seems almost naive—meditate on the law of the Lord night and day and you will flourish; follow the advice of the wicked and you will perish. There's a part of me that is tempted to preach against the text, to point out the holes—what about the sinners who flourish and the good men who are destroyed? But I know that knee-jerk reading is laughably superficial, tragically short-sighted. We are talking about eternity here. We are talking about the fullness of time. The fact of the matter is we do have choices, and there are consequences. We are on a certain path if we opt to turn our attention to truth and beauty and goodness—the law of the Lord, in other words. And we are on a different path if we opt to follow the advice of the wicked or take the path that sinners tread. That psalm is speaking the language you lacked as a child, my friend. It's not a threat, it's an invitation.

It's 6:07. Late for dinner again. I'm going to try to preach without notes, which terrifies me, but I am feeling a responsibility to trust that this psalm has made its way into my bones, and I should just open my mouth and speak.

I love you.

Peace,
Katherine

SEPTEMBER 4, 2022

Dear Katherine,

I don't mind the text thread appearance, but it wasn't necessary to prove your valor as a friend. Maybe "valor" is an atypical adjective to describe the character of friendship, but it fits. Not that a friendship with me puts you in peril, at least not these days, but that you charge into all my battles with nothing short of heroic courage. If there was a *Character of Katherine* series (do you think if we reference BibleProject enough that they'll give us a shoutout on one of their podcasts? Do you think it's lame that I would be beside myself with excitement if they did?), one of the episodes would be entitled "Tenacity." You may not have written a letter in a month, but you've been ever present in our relationship. Winn could probably play a drinking game reading these letters—drink when one author gushes about the other—and get hammered before he gets halfway through them. Cheers, Winn!

I want to talk about baptism as well. I don't know if your conviction about doing it in front of a congregation is as silly as you say, but I want to say more about my reservations. I am very into the second commandment, and because it's changed my life for the better in obvious ways, it doesn't particularly challenge me (yet). I can love until I'm blue in the face, but I'm not always comfortable on the receiving end. It's like that with help, too. Of course I want love and it's undeniable I need help, but accepting them can be hard. And asking for them? The most painful moments in my relationship with Ian have involved neglect in response to stated, pleaded-for, pitiful need, and there's nothing like neglect to communicate insignificance. He taught me to expect rejection, and inherent in a public baptism, standing in front of a declared community and asking to be let in, is the possibility of rejection. Heschel makes this beautiful point in pushing back against accusations that Judeo-Christians anthropomorphize God. He reminds us that "nowhere in the Bible is man characterized as merciful, gracious, slow to anger, abundant in love and truth, keeping love to the thousandth generation." Human concern for these virtues, he says, is a "theomorphism."[1] As Christians we strive to imitate the divine, but we often distort it. Frequently. I can't imagine anything but a loving reception at Covenant or First Congo, but my general fear of rejection is well founded.

1. Heschel, *Prophets*, 349.

Humans are not divine, followers of Christ or not, but I shouldn't dress up personal insecurity as theology. It's fear that holds me back from public baptism. Fear I won't be wanted, even though I have mountains of evidence to the contrary. I texted this to you today but it bears repeating, how welcome I've felt at Covenant. A pastor I'd never met approached me after worship, knowing exactly who I was because I had been discussed, and even as I write this my chest seizes up with emotion. With a congregation of hundreds, why would two pastors create room for me in their conversations? It baffles me that I would carry any import, when I am so small and one of so many. This pastor, David, engaged me for nearly twenty minutes about our mutual work in treating trauma, genuinely interested in my thoughts. It's been rare in my life to have agenda-less conversations with men, but it's the standard at Covenant.

I've had similar experiences with members of my small group, some of whom have gone out of their way to connect with me. We do prayer requests at the end of every meeting, and I am silent. You are the only person I've ever asked for prayers, and I could probably count on one hand the number of times it's happened. Maybe it's pride, but it feels more like embarrassment, like when someone asks you a question to which everyone else in the room knows the answer. Okay so maybe it's pride, but either way the whole concept blows my mind. For some strange reason, that night I felt compelled to talk about a relationship challenge, but I buried it in a reference to theological discussion from earlier in the evening. When we got to prayer requests, Matt, the group leader asked if I wanted some help with what I had mentioned, and I said something eloquent like, "Uh . . . I'll figure it out." He was not having it.

"Oh, so you'll just 'figure it out,'" he said; "You'll just deal with it? *Aloooooone?*"

"Fine! Fine. Pray for me or whatever," I said. And so they prayed for me.

He pulled me into prayer, and the kindness of it took my breath away. I needed those prayers, and badly. I still do, and so many, many more, but I would never have asked. I tried to opt out of community and Matt wrangled me back in. He didn't give me the option to suffer alone; he didn't let me reject love. Our culture obsesses over consent like the latest trend, and for good reason, but in that moment I needed care more than autonomy. I don't mean that prayer was forced upon me, but that my community knew what I needed, and it was going to give it to me whether I asked or not.

That's grace, and it only happens in Relationship, which brings me back to baptism. Maybe I should consider something communal. I don't know how I would square that, wanting so badly for you to perform the sacrament, but not in your church, which is not mine. I don't have a solution to the problem, but I will pray about it and we'll come up with something. I'm not in a hurry. I don't think God is going anywhere.

In the spirit of leaves that do not wither,
Devon

September 10, 2022

Dear Devon,

    I am presently sitting in my backyard. It's hot, but I'm in the shade of the house. Our yard is not particularly tidy, especially this time of year. I have a tendency to plant gardens in May and lose interest in them by September. We have more Creeping Charlie than actual legitimate grass, but I can't bring myself to care too much about that because it is green and enthusiastic; if you don't look too closely, it looks like we have a semi-respectable lawn. I have a scrappy strip of flowers by the side fence—well, flowers and weeds. I'd scattered a handful of wildflower seeds midsummer and didn't really know what to pull and what to water, so they all grew up together. There's a volunteer tomato plant in the mix, too. I never got around to staking it, so the tallest stalk fell over and off, taking the unripe tomatoes with it. But now there's a few fruits reddening on the vine. The only thing that tastes better than a garden tomato is a volunteer tomato—their unexpectedness adds to their sweetness. The back fence is presently the best, laden with a cloud of autumn clematis. The black-eyed Susans are gangbusters, too—we started out with a petite patch a dozen years ago, but they expand their territory a little more every season.

    And then, right in front of me: the redbud tree. It's often the tree I imagine when I meditate on Psalm 1. I did manage to preach my extemporaneous sermon last Sunday, thanks to the Holy Spirit. It wasn't the best sermon I've ever delivered, but I did feel deeply connected to my people (and, for that matter, to God). I told them I pray to be like a tree planted by streams of water, and that I pray for them to be trees as well. I could have preached a total clunker and it wouldn't have mattered much, because we'd all witnessed an exquisitely beautiful baptism earlier in the service. A family of four, baptized one after another. I wish I could remember where I read a reflection about baptism that points out how extraordinary it is that the name of the baptized is spoken in the same breath as the name of God. When I baptized the three-year-old in the name of the Father and of the Son and of the Holy Spirit, her jaw dropped open and she set her gaze heavenward. Oh, to have faith as a child.

    You've been in my yard once, very early in our friendship. You asked me to pray for you that day, and so I prayed—for discernment and clarity about a decision you had to make. It's probably one of the few times we've prayed aloud together—let's add that to our agenda when we spend time in Michigan next month. I am so glad your small group prayed for you, and that you let them. That kind of Christian community is invaluable.

One of the reasons I'm lazing in my backyard today is I rather wore myself out yesterday, cultivating that kind of sacred space for the folks in my congregation. First with Moms in Faith, and later with my new lunchtime Bible study (using videos from the BibleProject, of course). We are highly specifically transparent in our sharing of prayer requests, too. My heart breaks seven times when we go around the circle, week after week. But it gets uplifted, too—and not just by the joyful celebrations that are shared. I can't help but be moved by the expressions of care and empathy. Do you know the hymn "Blest Be the Tie That Binds"? It's one of my favorites, and I think you'd like it a hell of a lot more than The Hymn That Shall Not Be Named. The third verse sings:

> We share each other's woes,
> Our mutual burdens bear;
> And often for each other flows
> The sympathizing tear.[1]

I dunno, it sounds kind of schmaltzy out of context of the rest of the hymn. But I can't quit that image of bearing one another's burdens. I know you often feel alone, Devon. But when you are part of a worshiping, praying, loving Christian church, you are not. They are shouldering your burdens alongside you. Imperfectly, no doubt. But faithfully.

I have to laugh about your amazement at being discussed amongst the pastors of Covenant. You've certainly been discussed amongst the pastors of First Congo! I mean, thank God Meredith introduced us via email. In fact, I just went back and read our first exchange, about you joining our Bible study on the book of Job. I asked Meredith how you'd connected, and she said this: "She was referred to me by one of my seminary professors. I'm actually jealous that she's joining your group because I would love to spend more time with her! But it's the perfect place for her right now! She's delightful and she's 'zealous' [her word] in exploring her new-found faith and wants to do so in community. Thank you for welcoming her!" Lady, we were practically *fighting* over you! Not long after, I sent this to Rich and Meredith:

---

1. Fawcett, "Blest Be the Tie That Binds."

I finally had a chance to sit down for coffee with Devon Spencer, who has been attending worship and Bible study ever since a mutual friend/colleague referred her to Meredith and our church. She is wonderful—super smart, deeply interested in the life of faith.

We really connected and did have a frank conversation about friendship. I acknowledged that as a therapist I know she's never friends with clients, that pastors do have professional boundaries to tend, but that congregations inevitably navigate dual relationships, and that in our congregation there is affirmation and precedence for pastors to be friends with parishioners. I've developed friendships with many parishioners over the years but I can't recall quite the same immediate sense of kindred spirits, and especially since she's so new to our community I wanted you to know.

Of course, the subject for that email was "Prospective Member." I'm glad we both figured out pretty quickly that this wasn't the right church for you to join. There were very good reasons for God to send you here, but becoming a Congregationalist wasn't one of them. Anyway, I think you underestimate how pleasant it is to know and love you. I'm not the slightest bit surprised that your pastors and friends at Covenant have embraced you so joyfully.

I want to tell you one more thing about worship last Sunday. It was one of those rare days that included both sacraments. And, as the pastor who got the short stick for Labor Day weekend (just kidding!), I was responsible for celebrating both of the sacraments. Even though I'm not in a tradition that uses the title "Minister of Word and Sacrament," that is the pastoral office that has always resonated most deeply with me. So getting to baptize, preach, and preside at the table in a single Sunday is thrilling. That being said, I've always had a complicated relationship with the Table. I love Communion. But for years, as I approached the Table and opened my mouth to speak the liturgy, I've been hit by a wave of shame. Sometimes it's strong enough to leave me physically queasy. I've just never felt worthy of my role as the breaker of bread and pourer of wine. No matter that we begin that ritual with Prayers of Confession; I've had this deep-seated fear that I am disqualified by inadequacies and sin. Devon, last Sunday I did not feel that shame. And it's not that I suddenly feel worthy in my own right. I feel gripped by the grace of God—forgiven and free.

Today you texted me that the book of Revelation is blowing your mind. I've yet to read it with a straight face. It is a weird book, and has been read badly—even harmfully—far too often in Christian history. I'm really looking forward to reading *Reversed Thunder* with you. Your copy should arrive tomorrow.

And now, it is once again time for me to make dinner.

Love,
Katherine

September 11, 2022

Dear Katherine,

What a glorious letter. Descriptions of nature tend not to evoke in me little more than indifference, but the way you wrote about your garden tickled me. Yes, *tickled*. Honestly, I'm as surprised as one of us at the exuberance in my tone, because it has been a long fucking weekend, but your writing positively *tickled* my spirits. I wouldn't know a volunteer tomato from a bump on a log, assuming that this is in fact a type of tomato and not some sort of gardener code for something I have no interest in learning about, but I want to make a salad—a caprese salad—out of one of yours. I nearly wept for that poor, gawky stalk, gone from this world before its time, fruitless. I don't know what clematis are, but black-eyed Susans hold a special place in my heart. In my head, them going "gangbusters" looks something like the animated California Raisins that may have predated my birth, but nevertheless made it onto one of our VHS tape recordings of the Muppets. In any case, I imagined a cluster of preternaturally cool, musically gifted flowers bopping joyfully around the garden. I loved this paragraph so much.

And then, against all odds, the fun continues! Well okay, maybe not always "fun" exactly, but you get it.

Nothing could detract from the lusciousness of this epistle, but I have to correct your memory of our meeting in your backyard. I remember that afternoon well, because I needed something from you that day. I was beside myself with confusion and shame after turning down a job at a declaratively faith-based practice, convinced I had betrayed God himself. I can't believe it was only a year ago that the notion of affiliating publicly with Christianity sent me into paroxysms of anxiety. I am desperately grateful for how dramatically that has shifted, but I am so sad for that woman in your backyard. You were wonderful that day. You told me about your dark night of the soul, and your unbelief was a balm to my disgrace. It also had the surprising effect of allowing myself to claim my faith, to call myself by God's name. I need you as a friend, and such a cherished one, more than I need you as my pastor, but that day you were perfect in the priestly role. The correction I have to offer is that I did not ask you to pray for me. First of all, nothing could have been further from my character, at that time especially. But more to the point, I remember you asking if you could pray for me. Meredith was the first person who had ever done it and you were the second, and I promise you I will never, ever forget those occasions. I'm sure you witnessed my tears, but in case you didn't, know that it was you who brought them on. It was how my small group made me feel, but on steroids. Thank you. I love you.

Isn't it funny, how we don't measure our sins to scale? I know many of yours and how they've knocked you sideways, but I was surprised to read of your fears of disqualification. I can't help but compare my sins to others', and if our juxtaposition was a competition of ungodliness, I would win in spades—in volume and depravity. If we did a sin power ranking, I would blow you out of the water. And yet, I know that's not how it works. Since we're not Catholic (though as we know I am a Catholic sympathizer), a sin is a sin is a sin. I guess. Right? Pastor Dan said this to me once, but even he conceded that some sins feel worse to him than others. Sexual sin, for instance, which I consider the nuclear bomb of sins; it has the power to wipe out an entire family. But no matter my rubric, I shouldn't and won't qualify your sins. When I read that sentence, the prevailing feeling was empathy. My heart crumpled with you, and I so deeply felt your insecurity that I nearly missed your triumph in accepting salvation. The victory is in the acceptance, grace being so easy to reject, and I celebrate you.

My brain is failing me so I will end this letter for all of our sakes (Winn, you're probably so hammered you should head to bed), but first a note on Revelation:

Why on earth would you laugh at this book? Is it the dragons? The beasts? The angels with their summons? Is it all the horns, musical and animal? I have dozens of letters in me about the divinity of Scripture, but for now I will say that it saddens me to conceive of it as anything less. With humans as scribes it is inherently fallible, but divine nonetheless. How tragic, to imagine it as mere literary history. You didn't say that and I don't think you believe exactly that, but we have much to discuss.

You are simply the best,
Devon

September 14, 2022

Dear Devon,

Thanks for your kind words about my random backyard description—it makes me happy that it tickled your spirits. I think one of the things I love so much about writing letters is that the genre is so unrestrained. There's a form—address, body, complimentary close—but the body can encompass anything and everything. The freedom is sublime. If I want to describe my volunteer tomatoes, I can. If I want to marvel over the healing of my heart at the Communion table, I can. If I want to misremember how it went down when I prayed for you, I can—and I can also acknowledge that you're undoubtedly correct. I asked you if I could pray for you. I remember that day as one of the few I've felt awkward with you—unsure how to read you, uncertain how to respond. I was consciously trying to step back into a primarily pastoral role with you, and we were so new in our friendship I wasn't sure if I was doing it right. I think that might also be the day you brought me a big bag of fabulous shoes that you didn't need or want anymore. I would wear those red cowboy boots every day if they weren't so snug. As it is, they're worth squeezed toes every so often. I'm glad I was able to minister to you despite my insecurity. God is so good. God's grace is sufficient for me, Christ's power perfected in my weakness.

Speaking of grace: about those tomatoes! Volunteer tomatoes can come in any variety—Big Boy, Early Girl, Cherokee Purple (my favorites). The point is that they grow unbidden. They grow where they were not planted—at least not by a gardener. Maybe a cardinal deposited the cherry tomato seeds in my scraggly little flower and weed patch—who knows? Volunteer tomatoes are like grace—unmerited favor, undeserved glory. Honestly, thinking of them that way makes me feel even more terrible about failing to properly care for my little crop. All they needed was a rusty cage plunked down around them and they'd have borne so much more fruit. I need to be a better steward of the gifts I'm given. Or maybe I need to stop being hard on myself about not keeping up with everything.

It's not so much that I *laugh* at the book of Revelation. (Okay, maybe I've chuckled at the inclusion of the dragon.) I more *blanch* at the book of Revelation. There have been times I've found it so distressing I'm tempted to join Team Martin Luther, who did not find it worthy of the biblical canon. "Let everyone think of it as his own spirit leads him," he wrote in his preface to his translation of the book. "My spirit cannot accommodate itself to this book. For me this is reason enough not to think highly of it: Christ is neither taught nor known in it. But to teach Christ, this is the thing which an apostle is bound above all else to do; as Christ says in Acts 1, 'You shall be my witnesses.' Therefore I stick to the books which present Christ to me clearly and purely."[1] I'm not entirely sure it should have been included in the canon alongside Paul's letters to the Christians in Corinth and Rome, or Matthew, Mark, Luke, and John's gospel accounts. Which isn't to say there aren't parts of the letter I cherish; that closing vision of the tree is exquisite. And there may be no better image of God in the whole of Scripture than the one of God making the rounds with a hankie, wiping every tear from every eye. But the book has been so harmful so often; the lack of a clear and pure witness to Christ has made it dangerous when read irresponsibly. I'm genuinely looking forward to seeing what Pastor Eugene has to say about the book, and fully expect him to redeem it for me.

But even setting the matter of Revelation aside, the bigger question we're circling around is how we conceive of the Scriptures as a whole. What does it mean to say that the Bible is inspired? I certainly used to fit pretty comfortably into the liberal mainline, rejecting any biblical hermeneutic of literalism or infallibility. I was trained to read Scripture like an exegete, preferring genre and context above spirit and inspiration. I've landed somewhere else with my relationship with the Bible. I believe it is the Word of God, but that its holiness is really only accessible through the active participation of the Holy Spirit. Which is to say, I do think that Scripture is inspired, but that inspiration is a present experience, not merely a historical reality. Historical criticism isn't the enemy—in fact, I think there can be a lot to be gained by interrogating the context and genre of any given text. The Bible is, on one level, literature, and can be read as such. But there is also more, infinitely and eternally more, and the Holy Spirit alone can open our minds and hearts to encounter the Word. Does that make sense? As a preacher, I've always been fairly agitated by arguments about whether or not any given story happened as it is said to have happened in Scripture. I'm so much more interested in the meaning of the Scriptures—what is the Holy Spirit communicating through this Living Word? And I truly find these questions most powerfully considered in the context of community, where two or three are gathered in Jesus' name. It's why I keep on keeping on with my small but mighty Bible studies.

1. Luther, "Preface to the Revelation of St. John," final para.

Speaking of—I have some reading to do for the first gathering of the Gospel of Luke study that commences tomorrow. And a sermon to write. And, how about we read the first chapter of *Reversed Thunder* before we have our bacon and date omelets on Monday?

You're simply the best, too.

Love,
Katherine

September 16, 2022

Dear Katherine,

The book of Revelation may be one of the points of our theological divide, which does exist in spite of many similarities. Taking a step back, I think we would offer slightly different answers to your question of how we conceive of the Scriptures as a whole. I'm with you that an understanding of the context and culture of biblical authors adds richness and depth to our interpretation of Scripture, not to mention accuracy. I also love how you describe inspiration as a present experience, and something we actively engage in when we read these ancient texts. Knowing is not an exercise in consuming and regurgitating material; we must feel to believe. It could be that I'm misunderstanding your sentiments, but I don't believe a reader's present experience retroactively determines the holiness of the Bible. For me, whether or not the Holy Spirit guides you through the text, it is the inspired word of God. That's not to say it should always be taken literally (I don't think the authors always intended that), but that cherry-picking for holiness can unravel the whole tapestry. If Scripture isn't divinely inspired, why should any of us care about living by its precepts? Maybe I'm misunderstanding this too, but reading the Bible as literature sounds like the task of a secular academic, not a person of faith. Reading the Bible strictly as literature completely misses the point.

I started *Reversed Thunder*, my first introduction to Eugene Peterson, and I think I like it. I'm not sure if I'll end up swearing oaths on it like I do with Nouwen, Wiman, Heschel, and Kierkegaard's works, and I'm already wary of his assertion that "If the Revelation is not read as a poem, it is simply incomprehensible,"[1] but I can get behind much of what he's said so far. Primarily, he had me at his insistence that those who turn away from Revelation are "the same people who suppress fairy tales because they are brutal and fill children's minds with nightmares."[2] For this alone, I will hear him out. In the first place, Revelation is in the canon and for that if no other reason we must contend with it. You might disagree with its placement (I'm curious to know why, please write about it), but it is in fact placed there, right alongside Matthew, Mark, Luke, John, and Paul. This could be another point of contention between us, but I believe that as with so much other confounding biblical content, we have a responsibility as Christians

---

1. Peterson, *Reversed Thunder*, 5.
2. Peterson, *Run with the Horses*, x.

to strive for comprehension and not rejection. Nothing about Scripture is easy. Nothing is intended to go down like a spoonful of sugar. Even Christ, the Savior of the world, was tortured and publicly shamed before dying a slow, agonizing death of dislocated limbs and eventual suffocation hastened by the weight of his own body. The Bible seeks to challenge.

    I think it was Luther who encouraged something along the lines of elevating books in the Bible that present Jesus most clearly, but that strikes me as dangerous. I don't know where, but I am told it was St. Augustine who said, "The New Testament lies hidden in the Old and the Old Testament is unveiled in the New," and I'm with him. Christ is *everywhere* in the Bible. The promise or the reality of the fruits of his coming is the through line of the Old and New Testaments, and the challenge set to us as Christians is to uncover that everywhere—in his benevolent miracles as well as the Babylonian exile. Where Christ is not, where we see God responding to "fallen nature, twisted by sin,"[3] he still *is*. Prophecies of salvation electrify even the darkest of times. When we disavow or disappear Scripture that causes discomfort, we miss as much about Christianity as when we read it like we would a historical novel. What's the point?

    I'm sorry to you and everyone else that I suffer bouts of righteousness I can't seem to keep off the page. I hope you know I would never presume to lecture anyone, but especially not a pastor with literal decades of knowledge on me, about Scripture. I don't know anything. I don't even think the beliefs I expressed here necessarily run counter to your own, which I know to be rigorous and salty—not saccharine. It's that I feel protective of the Bible, and of this faith that has given me life. I feel like the mother of a struggling child, misunderstood by his teachers and peers as unruly or malevolent. I want others to love him, and this text, as much as I do. Of course that will never happen, not in the secular realm and not within the bounds of nominal Christianity, but I will continue to preach the goodness at the heart of the conundrums and atrocities. I still feel sad for that woman (it's me, the woman is me) who didn't grasp this mere months ago, and don't want others to succumb to the same misapprehensions. It's all good news, right? I think it has to be.

Apologies for the tirade,
Devon

---

3. Jones, "Embodied from Creation Through Redemption."

SEPTEMBER 18, 2022

Dear Katherine,

 I wanted to say one more thing about Scripture as poetry. Not that it's not, because much of it is, but that it's always more than that—it's never only a literary device. It's never simply "imaginative writing."[1] I'm more nervous about Peterson than I care to admit—to admit to you, because I know what he means to you—and I'm most apprehensive about his emphasis on "imagination." I know, I *know* you love this. I'm sorry. Granted, I've only read about thirteen pages of the man's entire canon, and I swear to you I'm proceeding with an open mind, but I can't get past his assertion that Revelation only makes sense as poetry. Likely I'm missing several points, and I am ready and willing for Peterson to disabuse me of my skepticism as I read on, but that sentence struck me as so presumptuous. Like of course one must read it as poetry. How silly to do otherwise. He's careful to say that poetry isn't a synonym for "frivolity," and it could be I'm unfairly and prematurely pigeonholing him, but I'm worried.

 I'm sheepish to admit I wasn't aware just how established is the movement to read Scripture as literature, or how disillusioned some Christians are with God's mystery, but my research about this has left me disappointed, incredulous, and desperately sad. Heschel takes great pains to dismantle the (to my mind, insipid) arguments discrediting the prophets' relationship to the divine. This isn't a dissertation on his work so I won't delve too deeply into it here, but I will reference one especially batshit view he contends with, because it is just that baffling. Evidently, some people have tried to rationalize the prophets' invectives as the utterances of "foreign agents or professional agitators." Heschel says, "Jeremiah's persistent advocacy of a 'defeatist policy' has led some historians to represent him as an agent of the Babylonian government who, under the cloak of religion and prophetic inspiration, carried on an insidious propaganda in the interest of his country's foes."[2] I mean . . . what? This is for real?

 Why are so many reported Christians so rabid in their disavowal of God's power? Why are they so quick to write off Scripture as literature, or miracles as metaphor? Why on earth would they prefer this to a God who can do *anything*? This isn't a rhetorical question; I'm genuinely curious as to why Christians would prefer a religion of rationality over majesty. I'm

---

1. Heschel, *Prophets*, 530.
2. Heschel, *Prophets*, 540.

mystified as to why anyone would sign up for all of this if they didn't believe in God's omnipotence. "I believe in God, but not in virgin birth"; "I believe in Christ, but not in the resurrection"; "I believe in prayer, but the prophets were ecstatics." I suppose logic is safe. We should all be grateful for science, but we've grown so accustomed to "proof" that we dismiss anything that scientific laws can't support. Why is that? What are we so afraid of losing in suspension of disbelief? Is it so simple as "I believe, help my unbelief" (Mark 9:24 NRSV)? I think it might be. I think unbelief might be the crux of all this dreary disenchantment. Whatever it is, it is desperately sad.

I don't want to denigrate Eugene Peterson, Katherine. Or rather, the anticipation of Eugene Peterson because the poor man has yet to offend me. It's not him, at least not yet, but that one sentence triggered in me a response to something entirely different, but familiar enough to generate this emotional response. Denying the inexplicable features of God amounts to secularization. That's fine for secular folks, but I don't want it from Christians.

Now I'm really done.

Looking forward to breakfast tomorrow,
Devon

SEPTEMBER 20–21, 2022

Dear Devon,

    Oh, friend. Where to begin? I read your addendum on Sunday night, past my bedtime. It had been a ridiculously long weekend, though full of glorious moments. I loved watching you sing with your new band on Friday night at that intensely Midwestern dive bar in Brookfield, and again at my church on Sunday night. In between those kairos moments of beaming lovingly at my kick-ass friend, I accomplished an impossible number of things. On Saturday I took my kids to a nature center to see axolotls, to a movie at the LaGrange Theatre, and out for a sushi lunch. Then, I was at church all afternoon and evening for our fall Confirmation Retreat. In between the sessions I led (on prayer, worship, and how to look up Bible verses as many of these kids never did Sunday School), I frantically tried to finish writing my sermon. I finally finished it on Sunday morning, less than fifteen minutes before worship started. I preached twice, then raced back to my study for a Zoom meeting of our Christian Ventures committee. Then home to scarf down lunch and take Genevieve to her softball game. I pulled her from the game early so I could make it back to church for Words and Music, which did not trouble her one iota since this whole fall softball program has been a joyless slog. Groceries were not gotten until right before Trader Joe's shut the lights off. All of this is to say that I was not at my best when I read of your apprehension about Eugene Peterson. I didn't scroll up to reread your penultimate letter, which contains necessary context to fully appreciate what comes next. I just dashed off this emotional text:

> *I will respond properly and fully soon—but I do want to reassure you that I think EP is far more in line with your theological framework for Scripture than you fear. I get the sense that you're conflating two concepts that sound similar but are not. There's reading Scripture as literature, like, studying it as one would any text. And then there's reading Scripture as holy writ while acknowledging that as written word, even divinely inspired written word, it has a genre. The BibleProject people are all about this. Naming when something is poetry or discourse or narrative or history. You can't begin to understand what is happening in the text if you're misreading the genre. Saying Revelation is poetry is not saying it's the material equivalent as Emily Dickinson. It's acknowledging that in this book, God's Word is being expressed through imaginative, metaphorical language.*

> Part of what makes this so important with Revelation and why he's emphasizing it so much is because it's a book that has been terribly mis-genred. People read it like a code or cast John as a fortune teller tossing out predictions. These misreadings make their way into pop culture through stuff like The Late Great Planet Earth and Left Behind. Like some sort of supernatural conspiracy theory. None of that stuff is compatible with the whole of Scripture or the inspired apocalyptic poetry that makes up Revelation. Does that make sense? I honestly don't think there's a theologian with a higher view of Scripture on my shelves than Eugene Peterson.

Like I said—I was emotional. I felt protective of my mentor in all things pastoral and theological, and focused more on defending Eugene's honor than attending to the content of reflections. You admitted you were emotional, too—low estimations of Scripture and apostatic conceptions of God leave you, in your words, "disappointed, incredulous, and desperately sad." (I am *very* glad I counseled you not to join my church's discussion series on Marcus Borg's *Convictions*; according to Goodreads one of the most popular quotes from the book reads, "The Bible is a human product: it tells us how our religious ancestors saw things, not how God sees things."[1]) It felt like we were awfully close to getting into an argument at breakfast on Monday morning. You needed me to acknowledge that you had explicitly said that your concerns weren't really about Eugene. That line about Revelation only making sense as poetry had triggered a constellation of concerns about biblical authority and theological integrity. The irony is I share so many of those concerns, and I still feel fairly confident that you'll find Eugene Peterson does, too. I read on ahead to chapter 2 of *Reversed Thunder*, and had to giggle that several things I wrote and reiterated over lattes, about not reading Revelation as predictive code and whatnot, were echoed on those pages. But that's beside the point. I'm beyond relieved that the tension in our conversation didn't swell into anger. Once I was able to set aside my defensiveness about Eugene and my anxiety about our ability to navigate conflict, I was far better equipped to hear what you were saying.

We are getting into the deep here, and it's intellectually and emotionally demanding to sort it all out. I think I need to back up and retell my story. I think you know I grew up as a nominal Christian, and had my spiritual world rocked by a series of encounters with Evangelicals. That faith never stuck, however. I was deeply drawn to religion, but was susceptible

---

1. Borg, *Convictions*, 94.

to disillusionment and disenchantment. Disillusionment, because even at thirteen I could tell that the Religious Right driving the conservative evangelical movement was, in a word, problematic. And disenchantment, because I just didn't seem to be able to make myself believe in a God who seemed to be a figment of human imagination. (I'm going to use that word, *imagination*, again.) When I encountered my first liberal Christian seminarians at United Methodist church camp, it was exhilarating—enough to awaken a nascent call to ministry.

I still wasn't sure I could get over my doubts. By college, I thought I'd become a Unitarian Universalist. When I started worshiping at a UU church, however, I was surprised to discover how much I missed Jesus. It was around that time I read the aforementioned Marcus Borg's *Meeting Jesus Again for the First Time*. I can't recall who recommended it, a fact I regret. I owe him or her a big thank-you, because it was exactly what I needed to read. The title was apt: I felt as though I was indeed encountering Jesus again, anew. By the time I closed the book I was researching seminaries, eager to dive headlong into the faith and church of this new/old Jesus. It's a cliché, but God really does work in mysterious ways. I failed to become a Christian by way of altar calls and sinner's prayers. It wasn't until I tried to enter through the gate manned by Borg that I found my home in the Christian faith. Borg was more of a Billy Graham for me than Billy Graham himself.

Still, I'm not precious about Borg like I am about Eugene. I'm grateful to him, but I eventually stopped reading his stuff. I wanted more piety and poetry. I continued to appreciate the way he could translate Christianity to be intelligible to—well, people who "prefer rationality over majesty." People who couldn't accept an omnipotent God even if they wanted to. And to be clear, lots of people don't want to. But for those who *want* to believe . . . I can't condemn them for plucking the metaphorically incarnate baby Jesus out of the bathwater of the secular age.

You know that my original doctor of ministry project was going to be all about faith in this radically secularized culture in which we find ourselves. I still think about this stuff all the time. In *A Secular Age*, philosopher Charles Taylor writes that this intractable skepticism is part of the "malaise of modernity." In an essay about Taylor, theologian Matthew Rose writes, we live in a time in which one is "never, or only rarely, really sure, free of all doubt, untroubled by some objection—by some experience which won't fit."² My new favorite theologian, Andrew Root, keeps writing books sussing out the implications of Taylor's philosophy on faith, belief, and doubt. I haven't quite worked up the intellectual fervor to read Taylor's brick of a book firsthand. Root helps me make sense of why, despite having dedicated my life to God and God's people as a minister of word and sacrament, my own creed is still often a wistful desire to believe that is a mile shy of certitude.

How does one come to believe—in God, in Christ, in resurrection—while snuggly ensconced in the so-called immanent frame? According to Root, this Taylorian concept is a "closed system; its constitution and maintenance make transcendence implausible."³ Even if one experiences a flicker of "cross pressure"—the intimation that there must be more than the material, rational world—it's not like God can actually show up. We are on the wrong side of a locked door.

But in the Gospel of John, the disciples are on the wrong side of a locked door, too, and God actually does show up. Jesus comes and stands among them and exhales the Holy Spirit onto their stunned faces. Just as I long to believe in the resurrection, I long to believe that if Christ could penetrate an impenetrable wall to reconvene with his beloved friends, he can do it again with the impenetrable barricade of the immanent frame.

This is where the imaginative poetry of Revelation sings to me. The apocalyptic vision of Jesus rolling in on a cloud is bananas. (Like I said, I can't read that book with a straight face.) But in that final vision, no one will miss the moment. The immanent frame shall fracture, and every eye will see it.

I want to believe. And I want the risen Christ to return on a Monday morning, because it would be so delightful for it to go down when we're out for breakfast. I can see it now, the cumulonimbus rolling in with its holy passenger (#imagination). At first glimpse of his form we'll break into joyous laughter. Knowing me, we'll have to take turns going to the bathroom. But we won't miss it. No one will miss it.

I have more to say, but this letter is too damn long and it is too damn late. I want to talk more about hermeneutics and the inescapable human tendency to read Scripture selectively. I also need to clarify that I don't believe that "a reader's present experience retroactively *determines* the holiness of the Bible," emphasis mine. But I do believe that the holiness of

2. Rose, "Tayloring Christianity," para. 9.
3. Root, *Faith Formation in a Secular Age*, 112.

the Bible can only be *accessed* by a reader through the present and active participation of the Holy Spirit. Does that make sense?

I remain your steadfast fangirl and covenantal friend.

Love,
Katherine

September 25, 2022

Dear Katherine,

God shows up all the time. Like this morning, when my beloved friend interrupted my moment of gut-wrenching sorrow with a declaration, broadcast to an entire congregation, of her joyful gratitude for me—*me*. God shows up all the time.

More after I sleep.

Love,
Devon

October 2, 2022

Dear Katherine,

On so many occasions since beginning this project, I've regretted my more impassioned letters. I just reread my last two, and weeks removed from their authorship, all I could glean from them was fervor and fanatical tunnel vision. Sometimes I write with the unrestrained ardor of an adolescent, but because the point of our dialogue is the dialogue, I can't edit out the oversights and underdevelopments. The best I can do is gather my thoughts and re-explain, which is what I tried to do at breakfast several weeks ago. For the reader's benefit I will reiterate here that I know Peterson takes Revelation seriously, that he takes all Scripture seriously, that he is not one of tepid faith. I know he seeks to invigorate the experience of reading Scripture, and that understanding Revelation as poetry takes nothing from the gravity of the text. I know all that. My scorn had nothing to do with him, and everything to do with my own fears and frustrations about a secular approach to what should be a spiritual practice, but I don't feel so defensive anymore. If someone wants to read the Bible primarily as literary history, or to take the lessons therein with a grain of salt, that's their prerogative. I think it's a sad practice that misses the whole point, but it shouldn't touch my experience of the text as holy, inspired, and timeless. I could stand to work on my humility, and I hope that's translating now.

What I want to address here aren't my errors in thinking, but the omission of the personal. I raved in those letters about the indisputable divinity of Scripture, but said little of the challenge in that conviction. Father Mike says that if it's in the Bible, God wants us to know it. To me that's unshakable logic, and while it doesn't make the uncomfortable more comfortable, it does render it impossible to dismiss it out of hand. Refutation of the Bible as a flawed creation of feeble human minds, shaped by culture and thus conveniently susceptible to obsolescence over time, does not make faith easier. To the contrary, belief is extraordinarily more difficult without the lazy gray expanse of relativism. There is no "plucking the metaphorically incarnate baby Jesus out of the bathwater of the secular age" for me. I know better than to read the Bible literally, but the closer I inch to orthodoxy, the more loopholes I close, and the more I see there were never any loopholes, but rather black holes of denial and elective ignorance. The binding that holds me together continues to tighten.

Because of who I am, because I've decided that God must come first, I stand to lose a great deal. For a time it was a phantom threat, one I took seriously but theoretically because the losses were bearable: casual sex, infidelity, self-serving ideologies. I've craved them but never missed them. In recent weeks, however, the two people closest to me have both made the future of our relationships contingent on shared values, and I get it. I really do. Dissonance isn't a dealbreaker to me, but in some matters maybe it should be. Child-rearing, for instance. I get it. What *would* transpire, if we played tug-o'-war over our children's upbringing? What would erode in the marriage if we disagreed about ontological fundamentals? And in our relationship, Katherine, how could you trust me if I disavowed your ordination? Would you stop confiding in me about your sermons if I didn't believe you should have a platform to minister in the first place? You've assured me of our covenantal friendship, but on some level that must be contingent as well. Without contingency we could be with anyone at any time, we could *be* anyone at any time, but that's an impossibility. Everything is contingency, even belief.

I've been thinking a lot about Abraham and Isaac. Ian invoked that story when I expressed not wanting to lose him over theological differences, and I haven't been able to get it out of my mind. We are called to take up the cross and follow Christ, and we'll all fail in the perfect execution of it but we should nevertheless kill ourselves to try. The anxiety I've been drowning in comes not from disagreement with this demand, but from allegiance; I am tormented with anticipatory grief for choices I have no choice but to make. Against what will I be raising my sacrificial knife? Against whom? In *Fear and Trembling*, Kierkegaard expounds on faith through the story of Abraham and Isaac: "If anyone on the verge of action should judge himself according to the outcome, he would never begin. Even though the result may gladden the whole world, that cannot help the hero; for he knows the result only when the whole thing is over, and that is not how he became a hero, but by virtue of the fact that he began."[1] What I love and hate about this is how true it is. I don't know where I will land. All I can do is follow my faith. What could be more terrifying than to relinquish all agency, even if it is to God? I too am in fear and trembling.

I'm not done here but I have to be done for now.

Devon

1. Kierkegaard, *Fear and Trembling*, 52.

October 14, 2022

Dear Devon,

    Goodness, in the past few weeks I've been to Cheyenne and you've been to Paris. And in a few short days we'll be off to Holland, together. Holland, Michigan, that is. I am beyond grateful that you accepted the invitation to go to the Doxology conference with me. I feel like when I asked you we were still brand-spanking-new friends, and it seemed a little ballsy to ask you to go on a trip. But now I can't imagine going without you—it's such a perfect opportunity to share my school with you since you are such a significant part of my doctor of ministry project. I wish more of my cohort friends were attending, but alas. I'm hoping you'll meet them at graduation. Will you come to my graduation in April 2024? Maybe the most covenantal of friendships are still contingent, but I have every confidence that I'll want you sitting there with my family when I become the Reverend Doctor Katherine Willis Pershey. Even if you end up not really down with women's ordination.

    I mean no disrespect to Kierkegaard, but sometimes I wonder if he spent too much time with the story of Abraham and Isaac. The fact of the matter is this: God provided a lamb. Isaac lived. And even when another beloved son was led forth to die, death did not have the final word. Jesus lived. Jesus *lives*. Rereading your letter tonight, I'm brimming with sadness at your anticipatory grief at the choices you foresee. At the death-to-self you presage. I can't argue with fear and trembling, but my own experience of Christianity—particularly in these past few years in which my faith is paradoxically getting deeper and simpler all at once—is less fear and trembling and more joy and contentment. As Peterson writes, "Christians launch daily into lucky lives—lives of amazing grace, surprised by joy, where they count blessings. They are not easy lives. They are not cozy lives. Christians go to work exploring and experiencing all the details of new life that Christ's birth, death, and resurrection pour into them through the Holy Spirit. They are not explained lives, making neat or perfect sense, but they are *good* lives, robust with a goodness the Christians did not earn. *Lucky*."[1]

    Devon, I don't mean to argue with your anxieties or diminish your dread. Jesus told us to take up the cross. But he also said, "Come to me, all you who are weary and are carrying heavy burdens, and I will give you rest.

---

1. Peterson, *On Living Well*, 19.

Take my yoke upon you, and learn from me, for I am gentle and humble in heart, and you will find rest for your souls. For my yoke is easy, and my burden is light" (Matt 11:28–30 NRSV). *Gentle and humble in heart.* I guess what I'm suggesting is that maybe your faith itself can be a heavy burden at times, one that needs to be set at the feet of Jesus. And, I believe with all my heart that God wants you to live a good life, filled with blessings and joy.

I think that's all I have tonight, but I am holding you in prayer and look forward to talking about all this and more in Holland.

Peace,
Katherine

October 17, 2022

Dear Katherine,

    It's funny to respond to your letter while sitting across from you at Lemonjello's, surrounded by college students and plates empty of vegan, gluten-free (who *am* I?), chocolate-chip-pumpkin muffins. I am so conscious of my age in this coffee shop, but I wouldn't be in my twenties again if you paid me. I was self-consciously irreverent, brash, and riddled with insecurities masked by affectation. I didn't love myself then like I do now, and I do love myself. People mistake my punishing self-standards for self-loathing, but I actually feel pretty good about the person I'm turning into. I am so close to appealing to Beelzebub for a Faustian bargain to improve my writing, but we all know what happened to Faust. God keeps trying to show us that our souls are priceless, and we just keep testing those limits. We are such children.

    You know who didn't need any bargaining chips for his writing? Kierkegaard. He actually spends a great deal of time in *Fear and Trembling* celebrating that all things—all good things—are possible with God. He insisted upon it. Kierkegaard was a joyful man, if his writing is any indication, and funny. He was severe, and he rejected marriage to the woman he loved, but I think he found a great deal of joy in God's blessings. He knows God provided the lamb, and so do I, but sometimes God wants us to go through with the sacrifice. Sometimes it's not our beloved child bound on the altar, but a relationship that threatens as much distance from God as it promises intimacy with him. It occurred to me that all of this hardship with Ian is God's way of taking me by the shoulders and shaking me until my teeth rattle. Maybe what he's saying isn't "Be patient," but "*Get out.*" I'm certain he desires a sacrifice, but I don't doubt that whatever it is I lose will be to my benefit. I'm anxious and grief-stricken, but I'm also lousy with blessings and full of hope. I might not get the future I want, but I'm sure I'll get what I need. It's hard at times to accept that promised rest for my soul, but I do try. Constantly, I pray, "I yearn to be held in the great hands of your heart—oh let them take me now. Into them I place these fragments, my life, and you, God—spend them however you want."[1] (I'm praying again, awesome one, Rilke.) Without fail, I am comforted.

---

1. Rilke, *Book of Hours*, 139.

This is a non sequitur, but of course I will come to your graduation. I couldn't be prouder of you for getting this degree, and no one could be more worthy of this pastoral education. Where would I be, had I not wandered into your Bible study last fall? I was teetering on the threshold of religion, convinced I didn't belong, and you swept me up unreservedly into your world—our world, now. I'm not prescient but I don't think I'll question your ordination. Nothing would make me more confident than a pile of Bible quotes to support my beliefs, but when it comes down to it, it's about faith. It's not only the Bible that edifies, but prayer. Not only priests, but the eyes to see and the ears to hear—*my* eyes and *my* ears. Scripture is divine and the church is sacred, but so is my own relationship to God. And why shouldn't he speak to me? Protestants believe in the universal priesthood of all believers, and I suppose I am one of those, at least for now, so why shouldn't I have faith in my own faith? It will take courage, but I have that. In spades.

In fear and trembling, hope and faith,
Devon

October 26, 2022

Dear Devon,

It's hard to believe that it's already been a week since we *left* the Doxology conference. It was such a gift to enter that space with you—to sing praise songs next to you in the pews of Pillar Church, to be equally spellbound by the wisdom of Samuel Wells, even to negotiate the gale force winds and rain that made our quarter-mile commute so treacherous. I really loved the whole thing. I tend to wear myself out at conferences; it's not so much fear of missing out as actual joy of being present. By the end of the last night I was bone tired and uncharacteristically peopled out. I regret nothing. (Okay, maybe I regret the ill-advised bar ramen.)

I continue to be perplexed that I've found a spiritual and intellectual home in the Dutch Reformed world of Western Michigan. For so long I've pitched my tent with the liberal mainline church. I'm actively navigating how to stay rooted in a tradition that no longer feels sufficient to me. In his address laying out the vision of the Eugene Peterson Center for Christian Imagination, Trygve Johnson referred to "the privileged lethargy and spiritual malaise of a Protestant liberalism that is dying from within for lack of a conviction and confidence in the resurrected and ascended Christ."[1] *Damn.* I have experienced that privileged lethargy. I have lived that spiritual malaise. I have known the internal death that emerges from ambivalence about the Resurrection. I'm still stunned that I'm not there anymore. Stunned, and grateful.

A couple of months before we started writing letters, I reached out to Winn. I wrote to him more as my pastor than my professor. I needed a pastor for a long time, and one of the great gifts of joining the Holy Presence cohort was the chance to have a pastor again. I made a confession to Pastor Winn. Not a confession of sin—a confession of faith.

My initial plan for my project was to write about the challenge of cultivating faith in the secular age. I was going to borrow from philosophers like Charles Taylor and theologians like Andrew Root (as well as from Pastor Eugene, of course).

I wrote about the ways that I failed to believe in God despite my ardent desire to do so. I wrote, too, about my fear. I've told you that in the past I experienced what felt like spiritual attacks when I write about sensitive topics.

1. Johnson, "Introduction."

I started this project fretting that writing about my struggle to believe in a transcendent God under the canopy of the immanent frame would sabotage what little faith I do have.

I told Winn that the joke is on me. I had started avoiding my project manuscript because in the few short months after I began mapping out my original project, my *doubt* was sabotaged. I started praying as I've not prayed before. I started ministering as I've never ministered before. Today I can honestly say I feel transformed from the inside out.

I've always loved the Message translation of Romans 12:1–2:

> So here's what I want you to do, God helping you: Take your everyday, ordinary life—your sleeping, eating, going-to-work, and walking-around life—and place it before God as an offering. Embracing what God does for you is the best thing you can do for him. Don't become so well-adjusted to your culture that you fit into it without even thinking. Instead, fix your attention on God. You'll be changed from the inside out. Readily recognize what he wants from you, and quickly respond to it. Unlike the culture around you, always dragging you down to its level of immaturity, God brings the best out of you, develops well-formed maturity in you.

I do not say this with arrogance, but amazement: *this is what I am experiencing*. I told this to Winn and months later it's still true. I am fixing my attention on God and, to my profound surprise, encountering God. I cannot unsee what has been revealed to me in the past year. When once I could not pray, now I cannot cease praying.

I recently found notes I took at an Ignatian yoga retreat in 2019. I was depressed and anxious, grasping for grace, desperate for wisdom. I wrote, "I am living in desolation," echoing the Jesuit language. I also jotted down lecture notes: "God is laboring from within everyone and everything to bring into the fulfillment of life greater fulfillment and joy. Collaborate with God. We can sense God in everything. Goodness, care, joy, knowledge—sharing in God. Walk through the world with great dignity." I wrote these words in my own hand but they were like dust to me. I could not believe them. I could not encounter the God who is God. Now these words all but sparkle like new snow on a cloudless day. They evoke a deep and enthusiastic *yes* when all I could summon before was a melancholic *maybe*.

And as for your last letter—I shouldn't make assumptions about Kierkegaard. I don't know when I'll get around to reading *Fear and Trembling*, but consider it officially on my list. I am always a bit sheepish about my lack of experience reading philosophy.

I do wonder if that same Romans translation that speaks so much to me might have a good word for you as well. You speak of making sacrifices at the altar out of fidelity to God. But maybe the invitation today is not to discern whether or not any given element of your life is meant to be laid down, but to "take your everyday, ordinary life—your sleeping, eating, going to work, and walking-around life—and place it before God as an offering." I think maybe you are already doing this. Maybe this is a way of practicing surrender and cultivating trust. Start with the ordinary so that we are ready if and when we are called to lay down the extraordinary.

(On a related note, I suspect you'll be reading Romans soon and I think you're going to love it.)

I have a matter of days to draft a paper about the same topic I left behind for this project—the challenge of cultivating faith in a secular age. Or rather, "pastoral identity or congregational life inside the secular age." In some ways I'm eager to get back to this topic—or, I suppose, to address it head-on instead of through the slant of letter writing. It's *the* crisis. But in some ways it still makes me antsy. I just reread the first thing I ever wrote about this stuff, back in 2017. It helps me understand how you feel about some of your letters; I cringe at how I interpreted Charles Taylor to my liberal mainline congregation. Toward the end—right after I quoted Marcus Borg—I encouraged my people, "Let go of the struggle. Stop trying to believe seven impossible things before breakfast. Rather, seek justice, love kindness, walk humbly. Practice letting yourself love and be loved. Entrust yourself to the mystery. Therein lies the path to rebirth in the Spirit. Therein lies the way of eternal life." I mean, I have nothing against seeking justice and loving kindness and walking humbly. I have nothing against love, or even mystery. (Do you remember who said that "to say that God is mystery does not mean that God is unknowable, but that God is infinitely knowable"?) But I cannot believe I forfeited belief. I cannot believe I counseled agnostic orthopraxy. Ugh. I mean, I can believe I preached these things. And I know I meant them when I said them. I think there's a part of me that knows I need to reckon with where I've been to have any sense of where I'm going.

Finally: I couldn't agree more that you have courage in spades. Irreverent, brash, and insecure in your twenties. Reverent, courageous, and grounded in your identity as a child of God in your thirties. Can you believe the miracles we're living?

    I can.

Love,
Katherine

November 9, 2022

Dear Katherine,

My mother is curious about God. She seems so interested in what my faith has brought me, and with the journey I took to get here, and I love that she wants to talk to me about it. Her experience with Catholicism alienated her from the church, but she's open now. To what I'm not sure, but she's curious. She asks question after question, and today she asked how I was able to believe after a lifetime of unbelief. The last thing I want to do is discourage her exploration, but I didn't have the stamina to explain something so mysterious that even I don't fully understand it. I tried, but ultimately failed to make sense of it for her.

It's not only that I don't have a tidy answer, though. The truth is I am so tired of answering questions about my conversion. I grow weary of being "interesting." I don't understand what others find compelling about my story, and I don't know how to answer the questions: "How?" "Why?" "What happened?" I don't know, I don't know, I don't know. I was lost and felt utterly alone, but I'd felt that for years. At the time the door opened, I had hurt someone I loved and been abandoned by someone who thought they loved me, but that wasn't why either—I had been down that road before. As I write about what didn't matter though, I remember what did. I remember the night when I ended things with Ian for the second or third time. I remember a tearful confession of spiritual apathy, a permanent condition of unbelief, made all the more despairing by a longing for what I could not reach. I don't remember how we got to God in a breakup, but I've never experienced a more loving ending, because what Ian said was "I'll believe for you." He said it, and something in me cracked open. I'm telling you, I felt it in my body, as demanding as hunger and arresting as pain. I felt loved like I've never been loved, and by a person who has never excelled at loving me. I think now that it was not Ian loving me, but God, and I will never forget that first intimacy. I went on to read electrifying books and develop relationships with other Christians who would change me forever (you are one of them), but all of that would have meant nothing without that promise: "I'll believe for you." Ironically, the person who made that pledge appears to be slipping out of my life, but the faith remains.

You know I'm preoccupied with loss. The threat of it hangs on every unsettling question I have taken it upon myself to answer—about sin, salvation, and dogma. I am in mourning before anyone has yet died, and I take to heart your urging to reconsider what it means to sacrifice. At least now I do. Maybe I couldn't hear it from you before out of stubbornness or severity, but I have been able to hear it from Kierkegaard. Surprised? I told you, he's not what you think. I shouldn't write about Kierkegaard as though I understand him, because of course I don't, not fully, but I'm going to try. I've been rereading *Fear and Trembling*, and in it he writes about the Knights of Infinite Resignation and the Knights of Faith. The Knight of Infinite Resignation willingly sacrifices that which he loves above all else and reconciles himself to the anguish of loss. The allegorical princess he loves but cannot have, he gives up. The Knight of Faith, however, is miraculous, because he renounces what he loves and embraces the pain, but then "he makes still another movement more wonderful than all, for he says, 'I believe nevertheless that I shall get her . . . in virtue of the fact that with God all thing are possible.'"[1] Not in the next life, mind you, but in this one. The Knight of Faith "lives joyfully and happily every instant by virtue of the absurd."[2] The world would call the Knight of Faith a fool, perhaps a lunatic, but by faith alone he nevertheless believes that God will return to him what he has lost. The Knight of Faith is Abraham, who inanely believes God will return Isaac to him after his body has burned to ash. "Faith," Kierkegaard says, "begins precisely where thinking leaves off."[3]

As of now, I am a Knight of Infinite Resignation. I will give up what I have to for God, and I tell myself that is good, but I haven't made that final movement of faith. In my last letter I wrote to you, "I might not get the future I want, but I'm sure I'll get what I need." This is a statement of Infinite Resignation, not faith. I don't know if any of us truly makes that final movement, and maybe that's because unbelief is so pragmatic. If I commit to the grave someone I love, I cannot breathe life into him again. I am not a necromancer, and people don't just come back to life. That would be impossible. It would be absurd. It would be categorically Christian.

I have a lot to think about.

Love,
Devon

---

1. Kierkegaard, *Fear and Trembling*, 38.
2. Kierkegaard, *Fear and Trembling*, 41.
3. Kierkegaard, *Fear and Trembling*, 43.

November 24, 2022

Dear Devon,

    I said it via text, and again on the phone, and now for a third time: Happy Thanksgiving, friend. I am not really that into Thanksgiving, to be honest. As I told my brother-in-law, I'm more into the Jesusy holidays. Give me the incarnational glory of Christmas or the resurrection narrative of Easter over a historically complicated secular holiday. I appreciate the emphasis on gratitude—I have nothing against gratitude—it just seems like God is so seldom thanked on this day. We lift up thanksgivings more generically—I am grateful for food, and friends, and shelter, etcetera. Grateful to whom? Just who, exactly, are you thanking? But even as I say this I am remembering the good old days when I was insufferably sanctimonious about Santa Claus. As it is, I celebrated Thanksgiving by turning my heart toward God in prayer and song at our Thanksgiving Day worship service. Congregationalists love Thanksgiving—hello, Puritans—and have some pretty kick-ass Thanksgiving hymns. Benjamin and Genevieve were ushering so I sat in the pews with Seb. As you know, I took a long walk while the turkey cooked, and then we had a simple but hearty feast with most of the classics.

    Two years ago I ran a half-marathon by myself on Thanksgiving Day. I was a mess, and all I could think to do was run myself into the ground. I ran six and a half miles into the Forest Preserve and turned around and ran six and a half miles back. It threw my lower back into terrible spasms. Maybe that's why my back was tight and sore today: muscle memory. That was one of the last times I was laid up with such pain. I'm going on two years without spasms, and there are truly few things for which I am more grateful than the miracle of living without that pain. All of this adds to my current agitation with myself—or rather, my current agitation with my body. I should be simply grateful that my body, which was such a source of suffering, has recovered. Instead, I fixate on how much weight I've gained in this past year. Lexapro has been so good to me in some ways, but there is a shadow side. I have felt overmedicated, alienated from my emotions. I don't miss being at the mercy of my anxiety, but I also don't really recognize myself. I feel heavy—not just in the places where I see the weight. I feel heavy when I run. I can't even run three miles anymore—not since I went on the highest dose. I feel heavy when I sleep. I used to need exactly six hours and fifteen minutes of sleep, and I felt great. Now, I often sleep more than eight or nine hours, and find myself unable to resist naps. So here I am, taking the risk of lowering my medication in hopes that I'll retain the benefits but lose the side effects. I know it's not that simple, but maybe I'll find some sweet spot in which I am no longer suffering in body, mind, or spirit.

Meanwhile, I am listening to the new translation of Brother Lawrence's *The Practice of the Presence*, by Carmen Acevedo Butcher. You might be ambivalent about some of her decisions; throughout the book, God has They/Them pronouns, ostensibly for the sake of the Trinity, but also for the thrill of praising a non-binary God. Still, it's a compelling book. Perhaps you have heard about Brother Lawrence, the humble dishwasher who developed a practice of awareness of God's presence and love. There's quite a lot about suffering in the book—he was a disabled veteran of the Thirty Years War, and experienced severe pain as he aged. So he was not a person who was unacquainted with suffering. But I suppose because of his elevated spiritual maturity and profound connection with God, he didn't perseverate on suffering. Nor did he anxiously pursue a "sweet spot" in which he no longer suffered. He prayed not to suffer, but to suffer well. I have never prayed for the strength to suffer with courage, humility, and love. I have only ever prayed for relief. Maybe this is somehow akin to Kierkegaard and his Knights. Like, the difference between resignation and faith.

I hate to break it to you, but I think questions about your conversion are going to be your cross to bear. People love a conversion narrative, and these days they seem rare. Deconstruction is all the rage these days. It's rush hour, Devon—and there you are, walking into the sanctuary just as so many people are fleeing. But I am sorry if all the curiosity makes you feel self-conscious, or if people want a tidier explanation than *I don't know*. Last week, when I was at the From Relevance to Resonance Writing Symposium organized by Andy Root, people were fascinated about my own transformation. They wanted to know how I went from being secular, depressed, and burned out to this state of renewal. Two answers are true: *I don't know*, and, *by the grace of God*.

I sincerely hope I see you soon so I can finally give you your birthday gifts. It was a joy to celebrate with you and meet your other friends. There was such a shared sense of gratitude that we get to be your people.

There is so much more to say, but that's all for now.
In Christ,
Katherine

November 25, 2022

Dear Devon,

    I almost texted this to you, and then I realized that I want it in the Record. It's that good. It speaks to your preoccupation with loss (which I think I share).

    "Console. It's from the Latin *consolor*, to find solace together. Consolation is what we do, or try to do, when we share each other's suffering or seek to bear our own. What we are searching for is how to go on, how to keep going, how to recover the belief that life is worth living."[1]

In Consolation,
Katherine

---

1. Ignatieff, "Art of Consolation," para. 3.

November 26, 2022

Dear Katherine,

You sent me this Brother Lawrence quote yesterday, "As long as we are with God, suffering is a paradise," and it's a beautiful notion but I can't agree. I spent the previous night FaceTiming with Ian, someone so well acquainted with suffering that even I, tragically gifted in the art of bearing witness to pain, lose my patience with it. It never sleeps, his suffering, and it gets its claws in me too. In any case, he was reflecting on the idea that God never gives us more than we can handle, bitterly rejecting it for a fallacy. His whole life has been more than he can handle, he said, and if his present station in life is any indication, he's right. His hell hasn't killed him, but it has prevented him from living. I know nothing of Brother Lawrence aside from what you've written here, but he must have been spectacular to believe that to anguish is utopic.[2]

I'm reading the Acts of Apostles and just finished Romans, and these men went so far as to "boast" of their suffering. Evidently they knew "that suffering produces endurance, and endurance produces character, and character produces hope, and hope does not disappoint us, because God's love has been poured into our hearts through the Holy Spirit that has been given to us" (Rom 5:3–5 NIV). I texted this passage to myself when I read it because it rang true, still does. If it doesn't kill us, like the old adage says, it will make us stronger, and hope can't disappoint us because the aim of it isn't to be realized in this lifetime—we have an eternity for that. I can swallow the idea that suffering is a refining fire that brings us closer to God, but I won't call it "paradise." It would be a betrayal for me to believe that.

What I do resonate with is Lawrence's (can we call monks by their last name, or do they always get the honorific?) refusal to pray for relief, and to rather ask God for "strength to suffer with courage, humility and love."[3] This is my way as well. An image that never fails to bring me to tears is of Jesus in Gethsemane, beseeching, "My Father, if it be possible, let this cup pass from me" (Matt 26:39–40 NRSV). This divine being, so utterly human and so very scared. That's all he asks, before qualifying that God should only save him if it is his will. Whenever I pray I think of this and it humbles me. If Jesus in the garden had the humility to accept his fate then so must I. Even when I beg something specific of God, I usually backtrack to ask for

---

2. Lawrence, *Practice of the Presence*, 50.
3. Lawrence, *Practice of the Presence*, 49.

endurance, patience, and strength. I know better than to superimpose my will over God's, and I'm not sure how I came to that. I think it's easy to acknowledge my lack of control because I never expected life to look a certain way, even as a child. Suffering has always been a matter of course. Things do not always work out. It will not always be okay. Not in this life, anyway. I don't mean that I shouldn't sometimes pray for relief, and I certainly don't think you shouldn't, it's only that it doesn't make any sense to me.

Don't be sad for me—it's a true comfort to know there's a purpose to pain. Sometimes, I think you find my faith too full of torment, and if that's true I would understand. It's hard to watch someone agonize when you know they have only to glance at heaven for a jolt of joy. I'm severe, fretful, and at my darkest moments, self-flagellating, and I'm not sure that I do feel the joy you revel in. I feel an abundance of love though, and peace like I never could have imagined in my atheistic past. Don't worry about me when I suffer, because while I don't rejoice in it, and it is assuredly not a paradise, I will continue to pray for endurance, patience, and strength. And wisdom. Always wisdom. If that prayer is ever answered, I can die happy.

Love,
Devon

December 1, 2022

Dear Katherine,

I lay in bed after writing that last letter, sleepless and feeling like a liar. We know I do this: I get on a tear and I write like a zealot, and it's not until the dust settles that the inconsistencies pile up like accusations. It's true that I try to hold myself to the Gethsemane standard, but where Jesus endured in his faith I buckle. In countless moments of desperation I pray for safety, healing, sleep, and even miracles. Fear renders me shameless in my requests, humility an afterthought to the pain I want so badly for God to ease, his will or not.

I've been thinking these past few days about how I could make such an audacious claim to humility, and I wonder if it's because most of the time when I pray for relief, I'm praying for others. Most often, I catch my own selfish prayers and start over from a place of humility, but I'm more flagrant when the people I love need relief. It's not because I'm selfless—I've never been stricken with chronic pain or mysterious illness, I've never lost someone I loved too young, and when I do I imagine I'll pray differently—but because the suffering of others seems so frequently to surpass my own. A friend whose IUI failed for the second time seems in greater need than I, childless myself and assuredly not by choice. You, supporting your husband as his family members succumb one after another to illness and in some cases death, are beyond a shadow of a doubt suffering more than I am today, mourning the distance between me and the people who love me but not Christ. Ian can hardly breathe under the crushing weight of his afflictions. I'm a magnet for suffering, a tractor beam for trauma, and it circles me as I live this charmed life. I have a darkness in me and sometimes I worry it will swallow me whole, but God has also gifted me with so much, nothing of which I deserve, and so I qualify my suffering and temper my prayers. Patience, strength, and wisdom are themselves plenty to ask for.

I don't know what to do about my prayers. I don't know if I'm "allowed" to pray for the cessation of suffering, mine or anyone else's. Nouwen's *With Open Hands* suggests there's really no wrong way to pray. He even encourages us to be honest about the trivial things we desire, on the grounds that God knows what's in our hearts anyway, so there's no point in dissembling. I love Nouwen, but I wrestle with this. Can't we ask God for too much? What if in doing so we run the risk of angering him, like a parent who snaps at the child who has pushed her just a little too far with "I want"? I need to be careful about personifying God too much, our image bearer yet unfathomable to our feeble human minds. I know this much—he allows suffering. He allows it, and sometimes he inflicts it. I know that, and I think the task is to accept it, but then why pray for deliverance? Why do we read countless, plaintive psalms that call out for God's assistance? I don't know, Katherine. There's so much I just don't know. I will continue to pray for you though, and Benjamin. For whatever it ends up being worth, I won't stop asking God to help you. Hopefully, he won't get too mad at me.

With so much love,
Devon

December 1, 2022

Dear Devon,

 I started to date this letter "eleven," but somehow it is no longer November. Time feels all wibbly-wobbly; wasn't I just in Minneapolis, devouring churros at Colita with my friend Andrea? And in the weeks since then, I've been to Ohio twice. Neither trip was part of the plan. It's hard to express how much Benjamin's Uncle Tim meant to him. He was stable, dependable, and unfailingly kind. The funeral mass was at St. Angela Merici, and that church was darn near full. Tim was a basketball coach—the kind who gets that the sport is simply the means to shape young people into good people. People came in droves to honor his memory; at the funeral home the night before, they waited over an hour to greet the family. It was clear that night that Mom was not well, and we knew things were serious when she didn't feel up to attending the mass. So it wasn't terribly surprising that she was hospitalized just a few days later. I couldn't bear to think of her in that hospital alone. I had to go until my sister-in-law arrived. I'm so glad I did. It's not like I actually *did* all that much. But at least she wasn't alone when the soft-spoken oncologist came to deliver the hard news of her diagnosis. Throat cancer is treatable, but she will suffer. And we will suffer as we witness this woman we love suffer.

 I feel like I should clarify: I don't agree with that Brother Lawrence quote about suffering as paradise so long as we're with God. I sent it to you because it stunned me. It's hard enough for me to imagine not praying for relief; to revel in suffering is a step too far. And yet. If my mother-in-law's hospitalization is incrementally less terrible because her daughter and daughter-in-law rushed to her side, how much more profound are the consequences of God's presence in our pain? There's an old Iris Dement song that sings of Jesus reaching down, all the way to the ground, and touching the pain. To me the weight of the incarnation is located right there on the ground. In Christ, God showed up with and for us. In Christ, God knows what it is to be terrified and desperate, with prayers penduluming between angst and acceptance. And in Christ, God redeems and reconciles and restores us, planting us as seeds of Resurrection.

 I was stunned when I read your words about my joy. I've always thought of myself as a particularly melancholic Christian, plagued by doubt and consumed by distractions. But I think you're right. I think I do revel in joy. Or maybe not revel, but I've certainly been wading in it. This is so new it still feels completely surprising to me. I can't help but pray that you'll join me in that joy, but as it is, I'm deeply grateful you know love and peace.

You write, "In countless moments of desperation I pray for safety, healing, sleep, and even miracles," and why shouldn't you? When Jesus taught us to pray, he didn't teach us to pray his Gethsemane prayers. We don't have to sweat blood to petition the Lord.

Eugene Peterson translated Matthew 6:9–13 like this:

> The world is full of so-called prayer warriors who are prayer-ignorant. They're full of formulas and programs and advice, peddling techniques for getting what you want from God. Don't fall for that nonsense. This is your Father you are dealing with, and he knows better than you what you need. With a God like this loving you, you can pray very simply. Like this:
>
> Our Father in heaven,
> Reveal who you are.
> Set the world right;
> Do what's best—
>   as above, so below.
> Keep us alive with three square meals.
> Keep us forgiven with you and forgiving others.
> Keep us safe from ourselves and the Devil.
> You're in charge!
> You can do anything you want!
> You're ablaze in beauty!
>   Yes. Yes. Yes. (Matt 6:9–13 MSG)

I love this—the original, and the Petersonian. The simplicity of it. The knitting together of humility and practicality. (I admit I kind of hate the way the church uses this prayer as a piece of polished liturgy instead of as a model for *how* to pray.) Jesus literally teaches us to ask God what we need; surely "our daily bread" is not only literally the stuff that is made from wheat, salt, water, and yeast. Sure, sometimes we do need courage and wisdom and endurance. But sometimes we need safety, healing, sleep, and miracles. If we are truly beloved children of a trustworthy God, we don't have to be ashamed of our childlike intercessions. God is not an impatient parent, but a perfect one.

So I'm going to pray that my mother-in-law is healed, and that we all have the strength and courage to get through this next season with grace.

I'm going to pray that I will get a freaking break already, and finally have a chance to plan the Family Christmas Eve worship services. I'm going to pray that Benjamin will be comforted in his grief, and that the world will be kind to my children. And I'm going to pray for whomever that ambulance passing by is heading to help, and for all of my parishioners in all of their joys and sorrows. And I'm going to pray that you come to recognize that there is no darkness that the light of Christ can't overcome.
Yes. Yes. Yes.

Love,
Katherine
    P.S. Yeah, you can't ditch the *Brother* in Brother Lawrence. ¯_(ツ)_/¯

December 8, 2022

Dear Devon,

    After I wrote that last letter I took my last Lexapro—at least, for now. The side effects were driving me nuts, as I've been kvetching about to you for months. In the days since I've been getting reacquainted with my old frenemy, anxiety. She is *such* a bitch, Devon. And one of my new anxieties is that my newfound peace in Christ, my latter-days capacity to pray at all—let alone with joy!—will dissolve as the medication leaves my system. What if I wasn't really experiencing the grace of God at all, just the satisfaction of serotonin? During the panic attacks I had in the summer of 2021 that finally sent me running to the arms of pharmaceuticals, I remember feeling totally and completely alone in the universe. At best, God was a figment of my imagination. At worst, God was a figment of my imagination that had dissolved.

    Yesterday morning I had a brief and ugly explosion of anxiety. I pulled it together long enough to teach my yoga class—oh, the ironies—and then I went to Rich's office and sobbed about All the Things. Today, though, has been kind of nice. I have cried no fewer than five times. I cried twice while reading *A Heart That Works* by Rob Delaney. I cried watching Lizzo give her acceptance speech at the People's Choice Awards. I cried watching a commercial in which an elderly man painstakingly learns how to apply a full face of makeup in private, only to reveal that he's only been practicing on himself so he can give his transgender granddaughter a fancy makeover before a family dinner. And I cried reading an email from a parishioner expressing gratitude and appreciation for my ministry. I can't lie: it feels so good to be able to cry again. It's not that I haven't cried in the last eighteen months, but it's been rare. And so many times I've vaguely known that if I hadn't been medicated, I would have had tear-stained cheeks and a runny nose. It's not like I want to walk around weeping all the time, but I have missed the depth of my emotions.

    Let me tell you, I am going to *bawl* when you are baptized. I am so happy you are making your membership vows at Covenant this weekend. And I am so happy that you discerned that you should be baptized by your pastor. Of course I would have loved baptizing you (and now that I'm off the Lexapro, we wouldn't have even needed to fill the baptistry; I literally could have baptized you with my tears). Like I said while sipping my lamentably terrible coffee the other day, I think I am supposed to be your friend who is a pastor, but not your pastor, and you are supposed to be my friend who is a therapist, but not my therapist. Anyway: I cannot wait to bear witness to you succumbing to the beauty of that holy sacrament.

    Oh look, crying again.   I love you.

Peace,
Katherine

December 18, 2022

Dear Katherine,

It's no joke, transitioning off a medication that lived in your body for over a year. It's said Lexapro is undetectable after six days of discontinuing it, but anything powerful enough to banish the kind of anxiety you endured will not go quietly. I can be conservative about SSRIs, but they made life livable for you and that's no small thing. I'm sorry this adjustment period comes with so much volatility as you're reacquainted with torment, but I support what you're doing. I remember an unintentionally caustic comment made by a friend of yours about preferring you medicated, and I get it, but that friend is not me. I lament your suffering but I won't run from it.

What I can't get behind is your fear that somehow serotonin was responsible for your recent intimacy with God. I'm sorry, but I can't accept it. "What if I wasn't really experiencing the grace of God at all, just the satisfaction of serotonin," you fretted, and do you know what I thought? It's not kind and I'm not proud of it, but I thought, "I told you so." At times it's felt like the weight of my faith has been too much for you to bear, like it's a load you need to lighten. Once you suggested I lay it down at Jesus's feet, and it's not that you were wrong, but it felt like you were missing something. So when I read that paragraph, so help me I thought, "I told you so." Christianity is hard, God frequently answers prayer with silence, and anxiety is part and parcel to belief in a story we'll never be able to prove. It's not that I don't feel joy, I do, but it's not the pervasive characteristic of faith. How could it be? From the jump, our religion has been about defiance. To be in the world and not of seems an impossible stricture, and not taken kindly by the principalities and powers we're meant to stand against. Jesus must have felt the full range of human emotions, but does he ever laugh in Scripture? I don't think so. Instead, he died an excruciating death, nailed to a cross, abandoned by his (male) disciples, crying out to a silent father who would not save him. Christianity has always been serious business.

Serotonin has nothing to do with God, and communing with him has even less to do with being happy. Isn't it to the contrary? "It is not the healthy who need a doctor, but the sick" (Mark 2:17 NIV). Praising God for tangible blessings is easy, but I wonder about the fortitude of faith in those who prosper. It's in times of trial we draw closer to God, when we remember we are weak and broken and desperately in need of his care, and it doesn't always make us feel better. When we are "scattered in pieces," or being decimated like "a house gutted by fire," we plead with a God who may or may not answer. Unbelief persuades us that we're clinging to nothing more than a lifeless idea. But when we are shattered and reduced to "all the pieces of our shame,"[1] nothing save God can make us whole. Nothing.

I won't glorify suffering—I don't understand that impulse—but the one saving grace is that from there, if we're wise, we have nowhere to go but toward God. I am not Peter or Paul, and I will not ask you to excavate joy from the bowels of your misery. I don't envy you what you're going through and I certainly won't fault you for making a different decision down the road, but serotonin can't be what keeps you close to God. At best it's too fragile, and at worst an outright lie. You don't need joy for prayer, or mental stability for peace in Christ. I hope to God you get both of those back, for it's a punishing life without them, but God is more startlingly real than any pharmaceutical could ever be. You know all of this, and more than that I think you feel it too. You write about the return of emotional depth, about weeping at the drop of a hat, and you know that God is in every one of those cascading tears.

I don't mean to be harsh with you, Katherine. I also don't mean to imply any of this is easy. Mine is a house of the most delicate glass, and I would never presume to throw stones. All I want is for you to feel hope, and to know that your anxiety and whatever doubt and angst that accompanies it doesn't have to alienate you from God. I want to tell you that it's all going to be okay, because it will be. I don't know what that means, but I know it's true. Not to fangirl over Kierkegaard again, but can we be Knights of Faith here? Can we believe that whatever you've lost will come back to you? I think we should try.

I love you, I'm here for you,
Devon

---

1. Rilke, *Book of Hours*, 137–39.

December 26, 2022

Dear Devon,

It is the second day of Christmas and the twelfth day of my personal Covidtide. What drove me to take Lexapro was my severe anxiety about Covid, and just a few weeks after I went off the medicine the thing which I had dreaded and feared so desperately happened. I was so sick, and so lonely. Especially after Benjamin decamped to Ohio for days in the middle of it to go care for his mom. My poor children parented themselves for days, because I was too sick to do anything for myself, let alone for them. Thank God for kindly friends and parishioners who brought us meals. It was hard to sleep or read, so I spent much of my time practicing Spanish on Duolingo and binge-watching a Spanish-language heist show on Netflix. I did pause for prayer. I found a liturgy in *Every Moment Holy* that gave exquisite voice to the way I was feeling: "A Liturgy for Missing Someone." I think I prayed it the day that I burst into tears three times, once for each time I briefly saw each of my beloveds.

> I willingly carry this ache.
> I carry it, O Father, to you.
> You created my heart for unbroken fellowship.
> Yet the constraints of time and place, and the
> stuttering rhythms of life in a fallen world
> dictate that all fellowships in these days
> will at times be broken or incomplete . . .
> I praise you even for my sadness,
> knowing that the sorrows I steward in
> this life will in time be redeemed.[1]

I've been reunited with my family but I am still so sick. Steroids and a mask got me through Christmas Eve, but the fatigue was so fierce today I was bedridden for hours. In truth it wasn't Covid itself that terrified me most; it was the prospect of becoming disabled by long Covid. That is the ache I am carrying to the Father tonight—the fear I am plunking down at Jesus's feet. I don't know if I will be better in a few days, a few weeks, a few years. I hate the uncertainty of this.

All of this is to say I read and am now rereading your letter through the fog of Covid. And I admit I am confused. This is one of those times I

---

1. McKelvey, "Liturgy for Missing Someone."

feel like we are describing a different faith, a different Christianity, even a different Christ. It's probably like that old fable about blind men describing an elephant, but one describes a tusk while another a ropy tail. They are all adamant about what they've felt, so of course none can convince another of the veracity of his claims.

> So, oft in theologic wars
> The disputants, I ween,
> Rail on in utter ignorance
> Of what each other mean;
> *And prate about an Elephant*
> *Not one of them has seen!*[2]

Neither of us has seen the Holy Elephant, it's true. And yet. I believe with all my heart that there is no Christianity apart from joy, that it is indeed the pervasive characteristic of this faith. I don't need to be told that Jesus laughed to trust that he did. I mean, he was called a glutton and a drunk. Jesus wasn't lying when he said his yoke is easy and his burden is light. It's true that you don't need joy for prayer, but joy is one of the gifts of Christ. The fruits of the spirit are love, joy, peace, patience, kindness, generosity, faithfulness, gentleness, and self-control. And what is confusing to me is that these were, more or less, the fruits of the Lexapro. It is harder for me to be patient and gentle when my body is wracked with cortisone and adrenaline.

It's true, Christ dies a grotesque death. He suffers and there is no joy in this. But the early church recognized the fabulous practical joke God played on the devil on Easter morning. Paul even taunts death in the tone of a schoolboy standing over the villainous bully in unexpected victory: *Where is thy sting now, jackass?* (I paraphrase.)

Everything that is broken will be made whole. Everyone who is sick will be made well. The anxious and despairing will dance for joy. The lonely and grief-stricken will be lavished with kisses. The Kingdom of God is already and not yet and when I imagine it now, even with the tightness in my lungs and the exhaustion in my bones, I am thrumming with anticipatory joy. I guess I do believe that whatever is lost will come back to me. We can indeed both be Knights of Faith.

That's all I've got tonight—that, and a great deal of love for you.
Peace,
Katherine

2. Saxe, "Blind Men and the Elephant," final stanza.

December 29, 2022

Dear Katherine,

 I'm so sorry for your fear. I'm sorry for your health and your stress of course, but also your fear about what will happen to them. Serious illness is too close a cousin of mortality to bear without angst; we are embodied creatures. I wish there was anything I could do to restore you to health or ease your woes, but I am familiarly helpless. I do pray for you, and though I believe with all my heart that matters, I know in times like these that prayers can feel like vapor.

 That's what I tried to speak to in the letter that so confused you. I reread it, and I still don't feel like it strips the joy from our religion. I don't for a second think we're describing a different Christianity, and certainly not a different Christ. True, I said that joy isn't the baseline state of faith, but that's because of the omnipresence of suffering in the world. That's not pessimism; that's a fact, and one which vexes you even as I write this. To say that life is suffering doesn't disqualify joy, but rather reflects the reality of the state in which we must seek God. Ours is a fallen world, a truism undisputed by Christians, and that means life isn't easy. Of course Jesus laughed, but it means something that it's never illustrated. Of course love, joy, peace, patience, kindness, generosity, faithfulness, gentleness, and self-control are at the heart of faith. Of course they are. It's only that fallen humanity does not default to such virtuous characteristics—we strive for them. What love and joy exist are by the grace of God, if we are to agree that all good things come from him, and if the New Testament scholars are to be believed, we fully realize this joy through suffering. I've said I struggle with this, but ultimately I was trying to make their point. Mine wasn't a balanced letter and perhaps therein lies the confusion, but that was a limitation of scope, not theology.

 I'm returning to this letter hours after its inception, still puzzling over your refutation of "my" Christianity. Perhaps the difference between your thoughts and mine, at least when it comes to this topic, is not Christ himself, but the way in which we see the world he came to save. My own adversity notwithstanding, I have spent my life swimming in a pool of others' suffering so deep I could drown. Christmas with my family is never easy, and on Monday I will return to work, where I will do everything in my power to help my clients heal from their own loving but all-too-human parents, from hellish marriages, from bodies that betray them, and from the demons who seek to devour them from the inside out. To an outside observer, many of these clients are thriving. They have good jobs, spouses, friends, and enough money to pay an expensive therapist for her time on a weekly basis. And yet. And yet they are flesh and blood, mortal and vulnerable to the ways of the world, and that world has done a number on them. Trauma can be the work of a moment or a complex assault that plays out over time, and the seemingly mundane can carve out chunks of our innocence as easily as a knife slices through soft cheese. It preys on us indiscriminately, and all the love, joy, patience, and kindness in the world can't fully protect us. Not one of us will escape without scars.

It's not that the world I see is a wasteland where children don't laugh and birds don't sing; God blesses us with so much beauty. This world though, in which flowers bloom and music exists and people like your parishioners deliver food to the needy, is also a brutal one. We die, Katherine. If we're lucky we live for eighty years and then we perish as unceremoniously as one of those blooming flowers. God doesn't grant us Noah's 950 years, and that's because we fucked up. God can make the world perfect whenever he chooses, and one day he will, but for right now he has chosen something different. He maintains order in the world, evidenced by the fact we aren't yet extinct through our own foolish choices, but he allows for tragedy and he allows for pain, and he wants us to turn to him in the midst of it.

I don't want you to hurt more than you have to, and I didn't intend to denounce medication. I was trying to address you from a place of having already made a difficult decision, not talk you into one. Protestants don't include Sirach in the canon, but it's full of wisdom: "The skill of physicians makes them distinguished, and in the presence of the great they are admired. The lord created medicines out of the earth, and the sensible will not despise them" (Sir 38:3–5 NRSVCE). God allows us to suffer, but he doesn't enjoy it. By all means, alleviate what you can. I wasn't calling for your suffering; I was only trying to say that God can enter through it. I was only trying to remember hope.

I hope lightness will soon penetrate these dark days,

Devon

January 6, 2023

Dear Devon,

It is Epiphany. *On the twelfth day of Christmas, my true friend came to me.* Thank you for visiting last night. I've been in such a vortex, realizing that the overwhelming fatigue and uncertainty of this post-Covid existence had also triggered a joy-obliterating depression. I've spent a lot of time lying in bed crying—you would think I'd have figured it out sooner. But it dawned on me like a—wait for it—epiphany. Or reverse epiphany, I guess, as it's the opposite of a brilliant light. It is a black hole and I do not want to tarry in it. So here we go again with the pharmaceuticals. Wellbutrin. May it make me well.

There aren't two Christianities, two Christs. I know that. I've read and reread, and we are in one accord on essentially all of it. Suffering and joy are equally real. I'm reminded again of the Wiman quote. (*Everything* reminds me of the Wiman quote.) "Sorrow is so woven through us, so much a part of our souls, or at least any understanding of our souls that we are able to attain, that every experience is dyed with its color. This is why, even in moments of joy, part of that joy is the seams of ore that are our sorrow. They burn darkly and beautifully in the midst of joy, and they make joy the complete experience that it is. But they still burn."[1] Equally real, and utterly inextricable. And, the telos of everything is God—salvation, redemption, resurrection. Sorrow no more.

I've been thinking about our vocations, how in some ways they are so similar, and some ways they are so different. I cannot imagine the relentless narratives of suffering you receive day in and day out as a therapist, especially one who specializes in trauma. And yet, I do some of the same things from a different angle. I've walked into hospital rooms to pray with the dying, and into living rooms to weep with the traumatized and/or bereaved. I am useless in so many of these situations; I am not there to fix anything. I don't even have strategies to help people cope. All I have is a tiny fragment of faith that God is present in these moments of extreme suffering, and that I am called to step into those places and bear witness. But I also get to stand at the front of the sanctuary with the groom watching his beloved walk down the aisle, and select which hymns will be on the lips of the faithful during Sunday morning worship, and randomly decide that

---

1. Wiman, *My Bright Abyss*, 19.

what my church really needs is an art gallery in the hallway by my office and I shall henceforth be a curator. I get to lean into the joy, and cultivate my tiny fragment of faith that God is present in these things as well. And, my God, I get to celebrate the sacraments. I get to baptize babies and children and adults and . . .

[Here, I interrupted writing my letter mid-sentence to order an art print of Isaiah 43:19 to send to the girl I baptized on New Year's Day; her mom told me she posted about her baptism along with that quote on her Instagram page. "*Behold, I am doing a new thing, now it springs forth, do you not perceive it? I will make a way in the wilderness and rivers in the desert*" (NRSV). It will come to her in a bright orange envelope, unexpectedly, and she will be reminded of her baptism, and, I hope, of the new things God is doing in her life.]

. . . and, I get to celebrate Communion. The liturgy starts in betrayal and brokenness but is transformed by the Host into the new covenant—love and forgiveness and the messianic banquet every table foreshadows. I think it might be these sacraments that keep me grounded in my maybe-too-rosy vision of the Christian faith. Not the ritual of them; the radical insistence that there is holiness in water and wine and bread, that in these ordinary essentials God is working ever more grace into the fabric of Creation. They are reminders of the telos that is the source of my hope and joy: we die, yes, we die, and we will rise with Christ and we will dine at his table.

I just read *Answering God* by Eugene Peterson for school. One of my favorite chapters was "End," which is, fittingly, the last chapter of the book. He writes, "All prayer, pursued far enough, becomes praise. Any prayer, no matter how desperate its origin, no matter how angry and fearful the experiences it traverses, ends up in praise. It does not always get there quickly or easily—the trip can take a lifetime—but the end is always praise."[2] He shows how the psalms teach this, implicitly. They are full of lamentations and anxieties and imprecatory outbursts—appropriately so, as life is full of reasons to lament and fear and scream "Fuck Covid" in the car, as I may or may not have done the other day. But each of the five books of Psalms ends with praise, and the last book ends with a cacophony of praise. And even right there at the end of many of the most ferocious psalms, you find praise. It's not tacked on; it's the inevitable consequence of prayer, as irrepressible as a sneeze.

---

2. Peterson, *Answering God*, 121.

I think this is all my Covid-addled mind can manage today. Thank you again for coming last night. You ministered to me in my suffering, and I am deeply grateful.

Love,
Katherine

January 6, 2023

Dear Katherine,

 I wish you knew how much consternation your confusion about my previous letters provoked. I couldn't understand what I was doing wrong, or what kind of two-dimensional Christ I unwittingly rendered in my fervor. My fucking fervor, always. I should probably make peace with that, because I doubt it's going away, but sometimes I feel like a precocious child. Hebrews was the book I read alongside Revelation as I finished the Bible, and this passage hit a little too close to home: "For everyone who lives on milk, being still an infant, is unskilled in the word of righteousness" (Heb 5:13 NRSV). I am that child. Milk sustains me, and yet I have the nerve to write about this ancient religion that I've known for all of three years. No one wants to hear about my personal theology. I'm digressing into my own self-consciousness when what I wanted to say was, I'm glad you understand me now. It's so hard for me to feel sophomoric in my exegesis. Another thing I need to get over, because the fact of the matter is that I am where I am. I didn't grow up with this. I'm gaining knowledge by the day, but I'm playing three decades of catchup and there's no way around that. If anyone reads this, I hope they know that I know.

 I'm coming off my first day of my second year of Somatic Experiencing training, and I wish to God I didn't have to help "fix" anyone's trauma. I don't think I want to be in this role, I don't want the burden of helping people heal, but I can't get away from it. I don't know how to answer when I'm asked if I love my job, because the answer is no. I don't love it. I don't bounce into sessions, bright-eyed and bushy-tailed, hyped up on healing, and I don't end the day feeling rejuvenated. I am tired. I am always tired, and I am always afraid. I live in fear that I am not helping anyone, and that my clients, whom I love in every sense of the word, are not benefiting from my care. At any given moment I feel like a charlatan peddling snake oil. I treat incredible individuals, and all I want is for them to be okay, and often they are not. Sometimes I think they need someone different, or someone better. Sometimes I think I should abandon ship, not for my sake but for theirs. I wish more than anything that all I needed to offer was a tiny fragment of faith, and all I was called for was to bear witness. It's therapeutic to bear witness, and you should know how much you're doing just being there with your parishioners, being God's vessel. It's so much, but it's not enough for me. I need to do more, and I'm never sure if I am.

We've been writing about suffering and I've been thinking about my propensity to be around it. I've been conditioned for it, but I wonder if there's something else. I've been thinking about Jesus and the kinds of miscreants he associated with, and I think I get it. I'm not equating myself to Christ in any way, shape, or form—if anything I'm a Mary Magdalene—but it's true that I've always been drawn to suffering. I'm used to it, and any therapist will tell you that's enough to generate a magnetic pull, but I also have more love for the broken than the whole. All of my education and training tell me that this is pathology, that I can't get away from what I know, where I'm comfortable, but I refute that. All therapists minister to the wounded, but it's more than that for me; I love the broken more. So very much more. I hope this doesn't unsettle you, one of my best friends and most beloved, but let me assure you that I pray for your health and will love you in it. The thing is, that even when healthy you will still bear the scars of your trauma, and I love those scars. I want to anoint them with oil and tears and wipe them with my hair. Maybe that's pathology, but maybe that's love.

I love you and I love my clients, and while I don't get to marry them as you do, I rejoice when they prosper. Or is it joy? I struggle with joy, and these letters make me keenly aware of that, but what I get when my clients thrive is greater than joy—it's more complete than that. I get to see them settle when they used to panic, cry when they used to freeze, and end relationships that have broken them down into unrecognizable pieces of their dysfunctional selves, and it's like nothing else in the world to witness. It's not joy, but it is akin to salvation. To watch these people rise from the ashes is . . . I don't have the words. There are no words, and there could never be. You can't imagine what it's like when a client, beaten down by their negligent partner and hollowed out by loneliness, demands restoration and gets it. Or when another client, literally beaten down by their caretakers during childhood, finds it within them to love through their implacable pain. I don't know if it's joy, I don't know if I feel that, but it's sublime.

What *is* our common theological ground? Is it communion? I know you cherish it like I do, and it's good to know we can always meet there, but I've been developing my own theology alongside our letter writing, and it's starting to diverge from yours. We are not the same, and I am sad when I notice our differences. Ian was the only Christian in my life, the only relationship with God between us, until you. You welcomed me into this world, and you legitimized my thoughts, my feelings, and my continually capricious exegesis. You have been a touchstone for Christianity and you always will be, but we are becoming different. What we share, however, is our love of communion. There is an addict in me, and taking communion feels like the healthy high—the high that rips through your entire nervous system, elevating you to the heavens and burying you deep in the earth all at once—I'd formerly sought through disreputable pursuits. There is holiness in water, in wine, in bread. I connect so deeply to communion that I'm a hair's breadth from believing in transubstantiation. That's how badly I crave it. Isn't it sad that we've never taken communion in the same service? My church does it every Sunday. I would love for you to come.

I don't know how to close this letter because I'm not sure of the spirit in which I opened it. I think I'm afraid of losing you. I'm afraid that we started close in our theology, and will end so very far away. I'm afraid we will be less. What does it mean, the direction I'm going? For us, I mean. Will you still want me around, with my wariness about "progressive" Christianity? Will you still want me around your kids? I still want you around everything, but I know it doesn't always go both ways. I do love you though, and I respect you. And I miss you.

Love,
Devon

January 9, 2023

Dear Devon,

When I got to my hotel in Holland last night I had to text you a photo of the room. It looks precisely like the room we shared at Doxology last fall. I almost felt confused when I dragged myself over the threshold after class today: *Where is Devon's suitcase?* I'm still so grateful I had the chance to share a little bit about this place and these people with you. And I'm grateful to be here this week, as it was not a given. This Covid fatigue and fog still have me in their hellish grip. I thought I was feeling a bit better this morning, despite the fact that I forgot my bottle of Wellbutrin and had to make multiple calls to work out the complexities of an interstate pharmaceutical emergency. I guess I overextended myself, again, because partway through class this afternoon I was walloped by another flood of fatigue. I should have just left, but I didn't think I had the strength to walk back to my hotel, less than a half mile away, and wanted to wait to bum a ride. But when Winn called us to sing a closing doxology, I started crying. Not from the reason I have in the past—how beautiful it is to sing that praise song a capella. I was just so ready to be done, to find my way to whatever shoreline I might find on the edge of that vast sea of exhaustion. I hated crying in front of my classmates. I know it doesn't matter, not really. They care about me and they are safe men with whom to be vulnerable. But I felt like a little girl.

Despite my pitiful state, class was electrifying today. Winn led the session, reminding us that before Jesus was led by the Spirit into the wilderness to be tested by the devil for forty days, he was baptized. And when he was baptized, the voice of God spoke: "You are my son, whom I love, with you I am well pleased" (Matt 3:17 NRSV). Winn told a story of a particularly painful experience of saying goodbye to his own son. He was overwhelmed with all the things he wanted and needed to convey to the child, and felt immense grief that their time living in the same household was finished. He told us that he put his hands on his son's cheeks, and barely able to speak through his tears, looked directly into his eyes and told him how much he loves him. He wanted us to remember that we are all that son; that God adores us so thoroughly he would take us each by the cheeks and repeat what we are already supposed to know but so often cannot hear or believe: he loves us so much he could caterwaul. In the Message, Eugene Peterson translates the verse like this: "This is my Son, chosen and marked by my love, delight of my life." Glory be. Winn warned us that if we can't hear this word, we'll bend to every other word—that we will exact great energy trying to get someone else to tell us we're beloved if we don't know it first from God. (I am half quoting and half paraphrasing; I'm a terrible notetaker.) Again, this all transpires immediately before Jesus is whooshed into the wilderness—driven by the selfsame Spirit that was just showing off at the banks of the Jordan. Winn told us we're all going to end up in the wilderness at some point—unless we try to run. But out there in the wilderness we will encounter God—rescuing us, and disabusing us of the notion that we can make it without help. We need manna, we need water, we need that pillar of fire roaring with wild truth and beauty. We need God.

I need God. So badly. I am in the wilderness and I hate it. I want a Get Out of Long Covid Free card, and it hasn't even been the requisite forty days to be officially long Covid. I have been feeling immense shame about how badly I am handling this. I am listening to Suleika Jaouad's memoir of her horrific odyssey with leukemia, and it makes me feel like a whiny brat. But I am so tired, and so scared.

I will have scars, however faint, from this suffering. For the record, I resonated deeply with your words about being drawn to those who suffer. I mean, you know my meet cute with Benjamin Pershey. I was like, *oooh, he lives in a halfway house and writes poetry about his failed attempts to get sober! Where do I sign up?* I listened to "Misguided Angel" by the Cowboy Junkies on repeat when we were engaged. And for years now, my very favorite Over the Rhine song is "All My Favorite People." Indeed, it's one of the songs I'd love to hear you sing sometime. There's a line that speaks to your anguish about feeling like a child in this faith:

> We are not afraid to admit we are all still beginners
> We are all late bloomers when it comes to love.[1]

There is nothing wrong with being newly born from above. And call it pathology all you want, but as far as I am concerned there is nothing wrong with loving broken people most. It echoes Jesus. The liberation theologians will tell you that God has a preferential option for the poor; Jesus is all about the least and the lost.

Still, it pains me that your vocation as a therapist who comes alongside the wounded and traumatized causes you so much suffering. I loved the new insight into your vocation, though I cannot help but lament what

---

1. Detweiler and Bergquist, "All My Favorite People." Used with permission.

an impossibly heavy burden it is. I know you are an excellent therapist. I knew that even before I had the chance to play the client in the session you recorded for your training. I may have only been playing the client but the insight and healing I received from that hour was very real. Your clients are fortunate to have you, and I hope your confidence that this is true is greater than your fear that it is not. I think that the most crucial thing is that you love your clients. (I think the same is true of pastors; crappy is the pastor who secretly despises her parishioners.) I know it's more complicated than that, and yet, without the cornerstone of love, what hope would they have of healing, even incrementally?

It struck me when you reflected on your response to the healing you witness in your clients. You resist staking a claim on joy, saying that what you experience is greater and more complete than joy. It made me wonder if one of our differences is the way we define joy. To me, there is nothing greater or more complete than joy. Joy is the consequence of salvation and the culmination of Creation. When Peterson says all prayer eventually is transfigured into praise, I think what he means is that everything in the universe is tilting toward joy. When Jesus was about to die, according to the Gospel of John, he delivered a very long monologue to his disciples. "I have said these things to you so that my joy may be in you and that your joy may be complete," he said (John 15:11 NRSV). Why do you think joy feels insufficient to you? Happiness, now that's a flimsy thing. Fun, but flimsy. Joy is so much more than that. Willie James Jennings says, "I look at joy as an act of resistance against despair and its forces. . . . Joy in that regard is a work, that can become a state, that can become a way of life." In full disclosure, I plucked that quote off of the website for "Theology of Joy and the Good Life," a legacy project of the Yale Center for Faith and Culture.[2] Those people take joy seriously.

I thought we had received communion together; at least, I thought you'd worshiped at my church on a Communion Sunday, maybe even when I was presiding. (In the denomination I was ordained in, every Sunday was Communion Sunday, and I still feel hungry and homesick when we just pack up and go home after the sermon.) At any rate, in my understanding of the Table, we are not only communing with the people in the room. We are communing with the whole Communion of the Saints. We are breaking bread with every Christian in every time and place. Even the ones with whom we disagree. Perhaps, *especially* the ones with whom we disagree.

---

2. See home page of https://faith.yale.edu/legacy-projects/theology-of-joy.

That's why it matters so much that we stubbornly insist that Christ is the host. He is the one who gathers us in, with all our differences, and nourishes us from the singular loaf that is the Bread of Heaven and quenches our thirst with the one and only cup that is the Blood of the New Covenant. You are not going to lose me, and I am not going to lose you, because we will always, always end up at that very long table.

Love always,
Katherine

January 14, 2023

Dear Devon,

My best friend Lara has a theory about friendship: you aren't really friends until you've argued. I used to hate this theory and resisted it with all my might. But then, eventually, we had our first altercation. We were both hurt and angry. It took awhile to work our way through it. But when we did, it became clear to me that she had been right all along. We were closer, the bonds of our friendship more tightly laced. We had another disagreement, a bigger one, almost ten years ago, and it was the kind of battle that bubbled up again at inopportune times. The hurt was deeper; the wounds needed more time and care to heal. But again, our friendship emerged stronger.

You and I are struggling. I don't know if I'd call it an argument, exactly, but there has been mutual hurt and anger. You referred to it as a rupture in our friendship. At first that language felt drastic to me, but I think it's probably an accurate word. You once told me that it takes a lot to offend you, and I know I have. Maybe a rupture in a casual friendship would be fatal. But ours is not a casual friendship. Ours is a covenantal friendship. I am not going anywhere. I trust that you are not going anywhere. I am going to lean into Lara's promise that passing through these waters will only make our friendship stronger. After all, she's only echoing the wisdom of the gospel, ever moving from pain to healing, fault to forgiveness, rupture to reconciliation.

I typically read the New Revised Standard Version, but for Proverbs 27:17 I prefer the King James Version, non-inclusive language and all: "Iron sharpeneth iron; so a man sharpeneth the countenance of his friend." We have both been sharpenethed by our friendship, and there is more sharpenething yet to come.

Love,
Katherine

JANUARY 14, 2023

Dear Katherine,

"Be angry, but do not sin" (Eph 4:26 NRSV), says Paul, and I'm trying. I am still angry, you're right about that, and I'm struggling to hold back the demons whispering in my ear, "Fuck. Her." I don't know if you know this about me, but I am capable of rage. It runs in my family and it runs in me, and it's only been in recent years that I've managed to soothe that part of me that snakes its way into my ear, into every nerve in my body, and urges me to burn it all down. Scorched earth is what I want in those moments. Not much gets me there, but when I'm there it's all I can do not to light a match and turn a relationship into a tinderbox. It's ugly and demonic, but when it's provoked I'm like a thing possessed.

Anger is a hard thing to let go of. It feels so breathtakingly righteous to be truly and utterly outraged, a foil to the sickening state of perceived victimhood, and I'll take it every time. I'll take it and feed off of it until it starts to feed off of me, siphoning off whatever goodness exists in me until I'm emaciated and brittle, all the strength of my anger atrophied away. It's not a good look, rage. I don't feel that toward you, I should be more clear about that, but the demons are stirring. I should also be clear that this ugly anger is a "me thing," something that's plagued me all my life, and not to be justified. It's a big part of why I wrestled so strenuously with God's anger in the Bible. I anthropomorphized God, which is a sophomoric move but probably one we all fall into time and again, because I thought I recognized in God a trait I knew intimately in myself and in my family. I was wrong about that. God is different.

One of the infinite, insurmountable differences between me and God is his propensity for forgiveness. He just . . . gives it. Granted, it took the sacrifice of his only son for that grace to fully manifest, but now he just . . . gives it. I, on the other hand, struggle mightily. I don't know if we've ever discussed this, but I'm not good at forgiveness. I "let things go," which means I move forward in relationships with people (mostly men) who make a habit of hurting me, but I don't forgive. I'm not sure I truly wipe clean the slate of the person who's neglected me, mischaracterized me, lied to me, or taken me for granted like it's their Goddamn job. I can't forgive them like God does. I can't wipe the slate clean, as though nothing ever happened. It's not that I don't want to—it's that I don't know how. There's something human in me that clings to the memory of transgression, gripping it tightly enough to draw blood from a stone. The therapist in me knows that's self-protection, but what I'm really protecting myself from is peace.

You texted me earlier to ask if I thought we will be able to move past this soon, and I answered you honestly: "I don't know." We are at a theological divide that transcends the academic, and from which there is no resolution. At least not in terms of agreement. I've tried to humanize myself and my opinion to you, but you respond with arguments I didn't intend to initiate, and information I didn't think I was refuting. I am at a loss for where to go from here. More and more it does seem that my opinion—my quiet, passive, contained opinion—hurts you by its very existence. I don't know what to do with that. If I don't change my belief, and I don't think I will, how will you reconcile with that? I've been angry, but not because you disagree with me, and my feelings about your belief couldn't have less to do with how I feel about you as my friend. I don't know if that's true for you. You asked me for reassurance, and I gave it, but repair isn't in my power here. That ugly, angry part of me lurks in the shadows to see if it's proven right, that you can't accept me. It sticks around in case it needs to deck me out in defensive, protective armor, but it's not here to launch an offense. It's you who needs to decide if you can live with my theology.

Love,
Devon

January 15, 2023

Dear Devon,

 Last night, not long after I read your words, I spent some time praying and pondering. I read a psalm. And then I read these words: "Salvation is God's determination to rescue his creation; it is his activity in recovering the world. It is personal and impersonal, it deals with souls and cities, it touches sin and sickness. There is a reckless indiscriminateness about salvation. There are no fine distinctions about who or what or when—the whole lost world is invaded, infiltrated, beckoned, invited, wooed: 'for God so loved the world that he *gave* his only Son.' God takes on the entire catastrophe."[1] And a peace came over me. This breach in our friendship is part of the catastrophe. This is good news, because it means that we aren't responsible for figuring out how to fix it. We don't have to save our relationship any more than we have to save ourselves. We are in Christ, Devon. Not just covenanted to one another out of our own idealistic volition about what it means to be good friends. Our lives hidden in Christ, as Paul writes (Col 3:3 NRSV)—our whole lives. And that includes this sacred, messy, beautiful friendship. Yes, I can live with your theology because our lives are hidden in Christ.

 I have been feeling acute hurt. If your tendency is toward anger, mine is toward anguish. Woundedness. One might even say victimhood. It's not that I *believe* beliefs hurt; they just do. I wish it were otherwise but I do not know how to make that intense pain go away. But I realized I have been bringing my hurt to you instead of Jesus. I am not going to do that anymore. It is my responsibility to tend to my own feelings. I cannot make them go away, but I do not have to make them your burden.

 I hope this might seem like a "third way" to you. It does to me. There is no resolution, but there is our shared faith in the reconciling ministry of God, in whom we live and move and have our being.

 All of this being said, I do not want to continue the discussion about these things. Just as we are tending the boundary of privacy, practicing discernment about what we do and do not include in these pages, I want to tend the boundary around certain theological disagreements that are simply too tender for my tender heart.

 You are my sister in Christ and I will not forsake you.

Love,
Katherine

---

1. Peterson, *Reversed Thunder*, 153–54.

January 18, 2023

Dear Devon,

I'm finding it hard to jump back in with a "normal" letter, after the tumultuous couple of weeks we've had. A dark night of the soul friendship. But there are things I want to share with you, so I'll just jump in. Cold open.

I am very glad I made it to Michigan for my fourth Holy Presence intensive, but it was a hard week. I suppose it was inevitable that there would be a letdown after the magic of Montana. My God, that was glorious. I do love Holland and was happy to see my friends, but being sequestered in a beautiful place together last year was pretty epic. But what really made it difficult was that I started the week so frail from this godforsaken Covid. During our first class on Monday afternoon I crashed. The kind of fatigue that makes me feel like I'm drowning. The kind of fatigue that makes me desperate for the shore of a sofa or bed. The kind of fatigue that I haven't been able to get through without weeping. It was awful. I got through the last half hour of class just bracing myself against the assault. I got a ride to my hotel not a quarter mile away, and as I bowed out of the opening night dinner at Hops on 84 East, Winn delivered my salmon to the lobby of the Haworth Hotel.

Of course this meant I was anxious about having more episodes. I walked as little as possible, bumming rides around town whenever possible. By Thursday I was starting to feel a little better, with one odd exception. I could barely hear out of my right ear. I assumed there must be fluid in my ear, or maybe even a painless infection. But since this Covid case has been anything but uncomplicated (remind me to follow up with the cardiologist), I figured I'd text Bob, whom you know from Bible study. He's an otolaryngologist and such an unfailingly kind and generous person. Did I tell you he made a chocolate stout cake for my family after Benjamin's uncle died? He's that kind of person. It couldn't hurt, even if it turned out I was just being melodramatic. I was not. He took it seriously, meeting me in his office on Monday morning even though it was closed for the Martin Luther King Jr. holiday. No fluid. He was calm as he explained that I needed to start a high dose of prednisone as soon as possible, because there is a window of time during which sudden hearing loss can be reversed. After that, there is nothing that can be done medically. I appeared calm on the outside but was frantic. I filled the prescription, downed the first six pills, and spent the evening at church meetings trying to appear calm on the outside despite my still-frantic state.

I had the weirdest dreams that night, Devon. Some of it has faded from mind, but for the duration of the dream I was beside an ocean that would not stop rising. Water lapped into the windows of our car as my family drove along the coast in a quirky little convertible sedan. The threat of drowning chased me all night long.

In the morning, I could hear.

It wasn't entirely back; the audiology test I took yesterday still showed some mild hearing loss in my right ear. But I think it is fully restored now.

I am currently listening to the First Nations Version of the New Testament and on the way back to church from Bob's office the story of Jesus healing the deaf man in Mark came on. *Ephphatha.* So many times this past year I have felt the staggering smolder of God's providence. Thank God for Bob. Thank God for prednisone.

Thank God for music. I can listen to my "Prayers for the New Year" playlist again without the sound rattling uncomfortably in my right ear. I cannot express how devastated I would have been to have lost the ability to listen to music.

I am incredibly relieved and grateful, but still a little shaken up. This whole terrible Covid saga has been humbling. So many people live with chronic illness and disability. I've read a good amount of disability theology, and I have some good friends who write and speak beautifully about living with disabilities. And you know how much I loved my parishioner Diana, who died last year after polio left her with lifelong physical maladies. It's not like I hadn't thought about these things before. I did a great deal of theological navel-gazing over my own relentless episodes of back pain. But I always knew that would go away. It would come back again, sure. But I wouldn't live there.

My anxieties about the possibility of long Covid have long been intense because it could at least semi-permanently send me to the "kingdom of the sick," a metaphor coined by Susan Sontag but I encountered through Suleika Jaouad. Last week I read her memoir of her harrowing experience of having leukemia as a young adult. To be clear, I am well aware that my four weeks of Covid and my four days of partial deafness in one ear is not equivalent to *cancer*. (Speaking of: my mother-in-law starts chemotherapy and radiation on Monday; pray for her, please.) There was so much wisdom in that book, though, and it was wisdom that felt unusually personal. Of the kingdoms of illness and health, Jaouad writes, "As we live longer and longer, the vast majority of us will travel back and forth across these realms, spending much of our lives somewhere in between. These are the terms of our existence. The idea of striving for some beautiful, perfect state of wellness? It mires us in eternal dissatisfaction, a goal forever out of reach. To be well now is to learn to accept whatever body and mind I currently have."[1]

I can't help but circle back to the work you do. I know it can be so crushing, to dwell with people in pain hour after hour, day after day. But your work is holy. You are helping people find healing and acceptance in whatever traumatic kingdom they find themselves inhabiting.

You, my friend, are presently inhabiting the kingdom of the rundown and sick-but-testing-negative-for-Covid. I hope that you make your way back to health, and that I am well enough to go see you on Monday. I shall give you an awkwardly long hug.

Love,
Katherine

---

1. Jaouad, *Between Two Kingdoms*, 274.

JANUARY 27, 2023

Dear Katherine,

I've had the most intransigent writer's block, and it's not lifted but it's been too long since I've written to you. A dark night of the soul friendship indeed, and I'm not rebounding with much elasticity. I think it's because we haven't seen each other since engaging in that painful back-and-forth, and the feeling that lingers in my body is one of caution. My fear has driven me further away from you in what has been a great time of need, and I'm sorry for that. I am looking forward to breakfast on Monday.

In the gulf between us, I have nevertheless prayed for you—for your health, for your family. Prayer is such a funny thing. Scientifically, it's a preposterous practice. How childlike, to imagine that a thought in one's head could change the course of adversity, let alone make its way to a force so unfathomably great that it has "given orders to the morning and shown the dawn its place" (Job 38:12–13 NIV). Before I believed in God, I scorned prayer as nothing, as vapor, and now it's my lifeline. I know better now how powerful it is, and as substantial as the ground beneath my feet. Unbelief still taps on my shoulder when I languish in prayers not yet answered, but by and large I can surrender to the mystery.

I have begun to pray differently though. I wrote months ago about how careful I was to pray my own version of the Gethsemane prayer, "not my will but thine," but lately I've gotten sloppy. Or maybe not sloppy, but bold. If God knows what's in my heart, there's no use in forcing it into a more virtuous mold, so I've been asking for what I want. When I do that, from a place of frenzied wretchedness, I feel like I'm playing chicken with God: "I won't stop asking; *you* take it away." I suffer paroxysms of worry that he will turn around and smite my temerity, but I've been told again and again that he doesn't work that way.

If I've grown more audacious, I've also been trying to quiet down. Screwtape, in his affectionate letters to his nephew, Wormwood, urges his pupil to "turn their gaze away from Him toward themselves. Keep them watching their own minds and trying to produce *feelings* there by the actions of their own wills,"[1] as this will hasten their delivery into the hands of Satan. I so often succumb to the urgings of my idol-worshiping attachment system, but God's voice is not panicked, desperate, or shaming, and

---

1. Lewis, *Screwtape Letters*, 21.

I am learning to discern one from the other. So far I feel a greater sense of peace, but it is early days, and I know that I am no different than the pitiable humans in Lewis's brilliant little book, who "do not desire [the nakedness of the soul in prayer] as much as they suppose."[2] It's frightening, to trust myself to a God "there with him in the room," but "never knowable by him as he is known by it."[3] Nevertheless, I listen. Right now, I am hearing God say, "Wait." It's not the climactic restoration of lost love I was hoping for, but it's a calm, clear directive, and I am praying for the strength to obey it.

With meditation on prayer comes reflection on despair, the foil to faith. Kierkegaard (bear with me as I yet again try to talk about a theologian too brilliant for my full comprehension) says that despair is sin: "Thus, sin is intensified weakness or intensified defiance: sin is the intensification of despair."[4] One of the ways we intensify this despair is through casting off our own unique, God-given selves in order to become something else. He gives the far-too-relatable example of a woman in despair over the loss of her beloved, whose keening is really for herself. "This self of hers, which she would have been rid of or would have lost in the most blissful manner had it become 'his' beloved, this self becomes a torment to her if it has to be a self without him." A desire to be rid of ourselves amounts to a desire "to tear [one's] self away from the power that established it,"[5] and the terrible task of claiming ourselves requires the ownership of our burdens. This shifted my perspective about prayer, but also desire itself. How much of what I want has to do with abdicating my very selfhood? Do I want to use my gifts to heal people, or to be "a Healer"? Do I want love, or to be "the Beloved"? In both pursuits I recognize a longing to remove myself from my Self, as if that is the antidote to despair and not the root of it. I don't particularly want to embrace my anguish, however tailor-made for me, but I see the sense in it. I doubt I would have the fortitude of spirit to explore this if I were, say, suffering from chronic pain or living on the streets, but from the comfort of my middle-class, Chicago apartment, miraculously healthy in body and mind, it seems reasonable.

Last night I returned to Nouwen, as I do when teetering on the brink of depression, and flipped randomly to the entry "Find the Source of Your Loneliness." He agrees with Kierkegaard, that "when you run away from

---

2. Lewis, *Screwtape Letters*, 23.
3. Lewis, *Screwtape Letters*, 22.
4. Kierkegaard, *Essential Kierkegaard*, 361.
5. Kierkegaard, *Essential Kierkegaard*, 356.

it, your loneliness does not really diminish; you simply force it out of your mind temporarily," but also warns that to dwell too long in it is to invite depression. Strangely, unnervingly if I'm being honest, what grabbed me the most was the conjecture that his own loneliness (he was writing himself through the most difficult period of his life) was linked to his vocation "to live completely for God," and therefore the "other side of [his] unique gift" of devotion.[6] I don't want a religious vocation—I don't want to give up on the possibility of marriage—but the idea arrested me. It's not the first thought I've had about it, but it was the first time I felt the tiniest tug on my heart. I'm afraid of that tug revealing itself to be the hand of God, claiming my heart as his and his alone, beckoning me to reciprocate, not as a child but as a bride. I'm so afraid that I can hardly stand to think about it, so for now I'll leave it there, and wait.

Love,
Devon

    P.S. I don't feel crushed by my clients' pain, not at all. To the contrary, I am comfortable with it. What can demoralize me is the self-imposed sense of singular responsibility for taking it away. I take seriously my role in healing, and there is a world of difference between effective and impotent therapy, but my recent existential crisis was brought on by identifying too closely with a savior. The anxiety of punching above my weight class was more than I could handle, and I thought I could alleviate it through running away. By some miracle I've been able to lay much of that down, and I feel again like I belong to the work.

---

6. Nouwen, *Inner Voice of Love*, 36–37.

January 28, 2023

Dear Devon,

I haven't had a fatigue episode in a week, and my hearing remains restored. I cannot wait until I feel well enough to run.

You wrote that Kierkegaard is too brilliant for your full comprehension, and I have to make a confession—your writing about Kierkegaard is often too brilliant for my full comprehension. Maybe it's because I haven't read much of his work, but I fear it's because I'm just not quite sharp enough to follow. You wondered how much of what you want has to do with abdicating selfhood, and posed these questions: "Do I want to use my gifts to heal people, or to be 'a Healer'? Do I want love, or to be 'the Beloved'?" I don't think I understand what the difference is, and I feel like I should. Since I don't understand what the difference is, I don't understand why one of each pair is acceptable and one is not.

Jen Pollock Michel is no Søren Kierkegaard, but she is a contemporary Christian writer whose writing I've found compelling, especially her book *Teach Us to Want: Longing, Ambition, and the Life of Faith*. She interrogates the role of desire in the book, essentially asking if our desires are trustworthy or suspect. Unsurprisingly, the answer is it depends. It's been some time since I read it, but if I recall correctly she explores the space between "my will" and "thine," and ponders how we grow in Christ so our desires and God's desires at least become a Venn diagram. She writes, "Desire, if it is to be trusted, is to be inspired by a holy vocabulary."[1] I loved this enough that it stayed with me. This is why we might pray to be taught to want and petition to be trained in our desires.

At the end of the day, though, I think Anne Lamott is right: all our prayers boil down to help, thanks, and wow (though I'd add a fourth word, sorry).

As thoroughly Protestant as I am, I have precious little framework for "vocation" as it's used in Roman Catholicism, i.e., as a calling to a vow of celibacy. Like, so much so that I also had to reread that paragraph to grasp the meaning. (It dawns on me that it is also possible that my brain fog hasn't fully lifted.) In my circles, "vocation" is used more generally—whatever it is God is calling one to do or be. Which I suppose could include celibacy, but rarely seems to. I reckon this is probably because few people actively

---

1. Michel, *Teach Us to Want*, 93.

desire a life of celibacy, and I tend to think God takes into consideration what we want. It is not my place to question other people's sense of calling, so I feel like I'm creeping onto thin ice here. But I will say that it grieves my heart to think about priests like Henri Nouwen living in loneliness for long stretches of their lives. To be sure, he found meaningful connections with his many friends; I loved reading a volume of his letters that was published a few years back. It was one of the books that drew me more deeply into the practice of pastoral letter writing. But I can't help but wonder what his life would have been like if he hadn't had to forsake romantic love and companionship to become a priest. I have probably never been more rude in my Protestantism, so I'll stop here. Suffice to say that when I pray for you, I pray that you flourish in life and love; that your longings are fulfilled; that your despair lasts only for a night and you find great joy in the morning.

I've been thinking about prayer a lot lately, because I am rereading Eugene Peterson's *Answering God: The Psalms as Tools for Prayer* with parishioners. There is a section early in the book that I loved and several of the participants were alarmed by: "Prayer is not a private exercise, but a family convocation. In the presence of God, 'alone' is not good. Summon Eve. Call a friend. 'Where two or three are gathered together in my name, there I am in the midst of them.' By ourselves, we are not ourselves. Solitary confinement is extreme punishment; private prayer is extreme selfishness."[2] Granted, Peterson might be a bit hyperbolic here, and a friend in my cohort pointed out that he does a better job of making this particular point in his other book about the psalms and prayer: "Solitude in prayer is not privacy. The differences between privacy and solitude are profound. Privacy is our attempt to insulate the self from interference; solitude leaves the company of others for a time in order to listen to them more deeply, be aware of them, serve them. Privacy is getting away from others so I don't have to be bothered with them; solitude is getting away from the crowd so I can be instructed by the still, small voice of God, who is enthroned on the praises of the multitudes."[3] In *Answering God*, Peterson's point is that prayer might begin in solitude but must continue in community; and prayer might begin in community but might continue into solitude. All of this is to say two things: It seems to me that you started your prayer life alone, and it means everything that your prayers were, in the words of Eugene, "integrated into the praying community" of Covenant Presbyterian Church. Now your

2. Peterson, *Answering God*, 18.
3. Peterson, *Where Your Treasure Is*, 6.

solitary prayers flow into and out of the prayers of that congregation. And as for me . . . for years, I really only had communal prayer. I wrote about my struggle to pray alone months ago, way back in July. Now I feel like I can stop kicking and thrashing and just float on the vast volume of communal prayers that has buoyed me all these years, and trust that the current will keep carrying me into little eddies that are perfect for solitary prayer. I never have to pray alone.

Tomorrow I am preaching for the first time in weeks, and Monday we will have breakfast for the first time in more than a month. So tonight, I will give thanks, because I am greatly anticipating proclaiming the Word at First Congo and breaking the bread at Courageous Bakery.

Love,
Katherine

FEBRUARY 11, 2023

Dear Katherine,

    I have been longing to write you a letter, but at first it was life getting in the way, and then it was death. It feels wrong to write about anything but the loss of your father, but about that there's nothing eloquent or literary to say. I detest platitudes and assurances in times of grief, as though "God needed another angel" ever made anyone feel anything but furious. I won't quote Bible verses about suffering, or even my beloved Screwtape, who speaks poignantly about its purpose, because you've already committed them to memory, and because nothing but love is any comfort in the face of death. Not words of love, but love itself—a husband's embrace, a dog's head in a lap—and even that can ricochet off a broken heart. I come to you empty handed and I am sorry. I am so terribly sorry for it all.

    No platitudes, I promise, but there was a passage in *The Screwtape Letters* that I have reflected upon again and again since your father died. Lewis borrowed it from George MacDonald, who describes heaven as "the regions where there is only life and therefore all that is not music is silence."[1] I never knew your dad, but I know from your reverent descriptions that he was a virtuoso. Who knows what God keeps and what he redeems in the resurrection of our judged and broken bodies, but I can't imagine he discards the music. I like to think this makes your father well suited to the celestial plane. I wish I could have heard him play, or even sung with him. I wish I could have met him.

    I don't know how anyone goes on without a parent. In a perfect world, which you and I have never known, a parent dies before their child. It's simply math. You would think we would be prepared somehow, when the chronology unfolds as intended, but it's not always the case. Both of my parents are still mourning the loss of their own, and with one exception, my grandparents lived long and fruitful lives. We can't ask for much more than eighty-five or ninety years, particularly when children, marriage, and a myriad of personal accomplishments decorate those decades, but loss is loss and death is death. I don't know if your shock has thawed completely into grief, but I do know that if it hasn't yet, it will. I haven't yet lost what you have, but I've been all too close to it, and yours seems like the kind of loss that changes the very essence of a person. Being a child is the most

---

1. MacDonald, *Unspoken Sermons*, 188.

fundamental framework we have for our place in the world, and that schema seismically shifts with the loss of a parent.

You said in your last letter that my writing about Kierkegaard is "too brilliant for [your] comprehension," and that's not even a little bit true. I have no idea how much of him I understand, probably very little, but what I think he was trying to say in the example I gave is that a renunciation of self must occur in taking on the mantle of "a certain kind of person" (quotes, mine). To be "the beloved" is to reduce oneself into an object, a two-dimensional definition of some*thing*. It is to remove the me-ness from the fact that I am loved, and to instead assume the characteristics of a thing that is loved. As "the beloved," I could be anyone, which is problematic because I am not anyone; I am myself. I am Devon, who is loved, but I am not "the beloved," because I am Devon, who is loved. There's something about death that renders permanent this qualification. The God that we believe seeks out the one wandering soul, no matter the multitudes that remain faithful. Our God, for some incomprehensible reason, cares about us as individuals. When we die, we die as ourselves. We can't die any other way. Some of us spend our entire lives striving to become someone else, to leave the Self behind, but God won't have that. He knows that I am not "the beloved," but a woman with thoughts and feelings and experiences that coalesce into a unique human being, incomparable to any other human being. When we die, all pretense falls away, because we cannot fool God. I find this so beautiful. Your father will meet God as himself, and that's all he needs to be. To be stripped bare is to be exposed, but more to the point it is to be loved in that exposure.

I haven't been able to hug you, let alone hear your voice, since your father's death last Thursday, and it feels strange writing you this letter. We can relegate it to the apocryphal canon if it seems more appropriate. It's just that I have not stopped thinking about you since that day, and circling back to the beginning of this letter, although my meditations on your loss are vapor, they are undertaken with love. God, Katherine. I'm so sorry he's gone.

I love you, and I'm sorry,
Devon

FEBRUARY 27, 2023

Dear Devon,

 I don't know where to begin. It has been twenty-five days since my father died, suddenly and from unknown causes. I have used words like *overwhelmed* and *discombobulated* to describe my emotional state, but they are insufficient. I have never been here before, and I am never leaving. There is no rewinding to the time before my father died, though I have immersed myself in every photograph and voicemail and video I can find. I can't redo our last conversation, twenty-six days ago. I had called my mom and can't remember anything about my conversation with her, but she handed the phone to my dad after a few minutes. They were at the Cuyahoga Falls Natatorium walking around the indoor track, which they did a couple times a week before picking up my nephew at the high school across the street. My dad had just had his first iron infusion the day before, and he wasn't feeling any better yet. His hemoglobin had been haywire for weeks, so low another hematologist might have given him a blood transfusion. How far do I wander down the path of "what if he'd been given the blood transfusion"? Or down the parallel one, on which I Google things like "Can iron infusions be fatal?" I am drifting away from the point: during our last conversation, my father did this thing where he gives—*gave*—a verbal inventory of the matter at hand. He used to do this about the weather, describing in detail how much precipitation was expected or whether or not they would have to wear coats on the golf course. More often, though, he would rattle off his upcoming rehearsals and gigs. I always reacted to these conversations with mild exasperation. Was I supposed to remember what he was doing next Thursday? And isn't there anything more interesting to talk about than the temperature outside? During that last conversation, though, he was telling me about all the medications he had to take each day. Maybe that was the clue. I should have known, but I did not know. He was eighty-two-and-a-half years old, but he still seemed boyish in his enthusiasms and, bloodwork notwithstanding, remarkably healthy. My mother (eighty; but still runs three miles regularly and takes kickboxing classes) texted me an emoji of a groundhog that morning, and then just a couple of hours later she is calling me to tell me that my father has died.

 I am not quite done being stunned. In part because my father's unexpected death hasn't been the only calamity we're absorbing. Benjamin was already in Ohio when it happened because he was taking care of his mother. They were on their way to her radiation appointment when I called, so hysterical I could hardly convey the message. Radiation is quick; Benjamin made it to the hospital on the other side of Cleveland to sit with my mother and sister and the dead body of my father. It turns out that my mother-in-law wasn't just feeling fatigued and coughing nonstop from cancer and chemo; she had Covid, and soon enough, Benjamin and Seb did, too. One day, when I am less raw, I am going to laugh bitterly about the irony that just as I was unable to be at Benjamin's side for his father's funeral, nine months later he was unable to be at my side for my father's funeral. Thank God no one else got Covid—not me, not my mother or sisters, not Genevieve. I must still be immune, because I kissed Benjamin goodbye when he left to take the kids home for the week, fully intending to return for the services. Genevieve no doubt would have contracted it too, if not for the extraordinarily generous church family that took her in for the week. Anne has been in the hospital for three weeks now, and it seems unlikely she will be well enough to resume treatment. Every day another affliction is added to her medical chart—pneumonia, thrush, sepsis, etcetera. Meanwhile, Benjamin's cluster headaches have returned, and I threw my back out for the first time in two years. The first time in more than twenty years of marriage that both of our horrifically painful conditions have hit at the same time! (The dog also had surgery to remove a massive growth, and the car broke down in the middle of the road, but I feel like adding these more pedestrian problems is almost too maudlin.)

But maybe part of the reason I am not quite done being stunned is because I am stunned for other reasons, too. The kindness of the family that embraced my ridiculously Covid-exposed-yet-testing-negative kid is one of myriad kindnesses my family and I have received in these past twenty-five days. I feel cocooned in prayer. And I feel God's presence almost palpably. I am heartbroken but I am not forsaken, not even a little. We've received so many meals, so many hugs, so many sympathy cards. Rich drove all the way from Western Springs, Illinois, to Stow, Ohio, to lead the memorial service. My childhood friend Anna came from Indianapolis and was my "person" in the absence of Benjamin. The calling hours went on for hours, so many people came to honor and remember my dad.

You offered to come, too, and it's not like I wouldn't have wanted you there but I didn't need you at that moment; I needed you most of all after the fact, when we finally managed to meet at Courageous Bakery again.

I needed that long wonderful hug, and your generosity in treating me to breakfast tacos. I needed your letter and I need to write this letter, even though I still don't have the foggiest clue how to compose these words, despite the fact that sentence after sentence is materializing on the digital page.

Writing came easier when I was still in shock. I desperately loved the eulogy I wrote for my father—I knew that I had to do it, and I knew that I could do it. As agonizing as it was to weep through it when I read it at the memorial service, it was precisely what I needed to do. Much as I've always held myself to the standard that I will believe every word I preach, I made a commitment to myself that I would mean everything I said in the eulogy. The amazing thing is that I did. I do. My relationship with my father was complicated at times. I was too damn much for him when I was a kid, and I knew it, and that hurt. But I have done so much work to heal and forgive and accept and restore, especially in these last few years. I loved him, and he loved me, and the miracle of his death is that it seems love is all that's left. I don't have any more anger or resentment. I would give anything to feel that familiar exasperation once more, but that's gone too. There will never be another opportunity to roll my eyes at the shit he would forward me via email (two days before he died: *28 Ways Your Pet Is Trying to Say "I Love You"*). I just have love.

And grief. So much grief. Grief unlike anything I have ever experienced. It's been especially vibrant at nighttime. I wake up so sad in the middle of the night. The other night, when I was struggling to get back to sleep at 3 a.m., I started listening to an episode of *All There Is* with Anderson Cooper. I don't watch television news so I barely know who Anderson Cooper is, but, my God, it is an extraordinary podcast. All about grief. It had been months since I listened to his conversation with Stephen Colbert (who is, you may know, deeply religious and very acquainted with grief). But I've been working my way through it now that I am acutely grieving. The one I listened to in the middle of the night was a conversation with Kirsten Johnson, the director of *Dick Johnson Is Dead*. I will absolutely be watching that movie as soon as possible; it's a documentary about her father's impending death, who is not in fact dead but rather has dementia. In the middle of the episode, she calls her dad and he tells her repeatedly how much he loves her. And I just broke. I cried so hard I woke Benjamin up; he might have assumed we were experiencing an earthquake, the bed was shaking so violently.

If I keep going I will start crying again. And I can't. Not right now. I have to make dinner and take Genevieve to her guitar lesson. Life goes on in the wake of death.

I love you, and I am so grateful for all of your love and support and prayers.

Love,
Katherine

MARCH 20, 2023

Dear Devon,

    Yesterday morning I went to the early worship service at my church. Nearly the whole service was in song: Howard Goodall's contemporary requiem, *Eternal Light*. It was glorious and moving and I listened to the whole thing on the verge of tears. I am grieving my father so deeply.

    And then I slipped out before the benediction and raced to Covenant Presbyterian Church in Chicago, where I witnessed your baptism. It was a moment of such resonance and significance. Your pastor spoke eloquently about the weight of the Apostles' Creed, emblazoned in brass on the intricate baptistry. You responded to the questions for the candidate with confidence. When you knelt for the sacrament, I had to lean to my right so I could see what was happening—your mom and I should have been bolder in our seat selection, claiming a pew closer to the front. But I could see relatively well as Pastor Dan dipped his hand into the water and touched it to your forehead, once for each Person of the Trinity.

    I was reminded of those beautiful words from Marilynne Robinson's *Gilead*, when John Ames is reflecting on baptism. "When I was in seminary I used to go sometimes to watch the Baptists down at the river. It was something to see the preacher lifting the one who was being baptized up out of the water and the water pouring off the garments and the hair. It did look like a birth or a resurrection. For us the water just heightens the touch of the pastor's hand on the sweet bones of the head, sort of like making an electrical connection. I've always loved to baptize people, though I have sometimes wished there were more shimmer and splash involved in the way we go about it."[1] Maybe there wasn't a lot of outward shimmer and splash as Pastor Dan pressed his dripping thumb against your temple, but if untold angels can dance on the head of a pin, surely the Holy Spirit was waltzing in the baptistry. There is nothing quite so joyous as the baptism of a beloved daughter of God.

    I was, in fact, thinking about waltzes during worship. The song of confession was in three-quarter time—waltz time. It's a kicky time signature for a confessional prayer, but I loved it. I loved all the music in the service, especially since you were one of the song leaders. But I especially loved that waltzy song of confession with its vivid invitation to hide in the love of

---

1. Robinson, *Gilead*, 73.

Christ. As we prayed, I squirreled myself away in God's love and confessed my shame: I could not suppress my envy of the pastor's hand on the sweet bones of your head. I know very well you needed to be baptized by Pastor Dan. But there was a part of me that grieved that you did not need to be baptized by Pastor Katherine. And, since I am still burrowing my face into the hem of Jesus's cloak, a further confession: There was a part of me that felt like a foreigner in that beautiful sanctuary—an ordained woman among people who do not believe in the ordination of women. I hated myself for feeling anything but unmitigated joy on the day of your baptism. I know that my Hiding Place forgives me, but I hope you can too.

All that talk about waltzes triggered a memory from when I was fifteen, at church camp at Lakeside Chautauqua. I was struggling mightily with doubt—I wanted to believe in God so badly, but felt so intractably secular. On Thursday night of camp we had chapel service, including Eucharist. I had received the bread and juice and was kneeling at the altar trying to pray. Partway through my prayer, the music changed from something somber to something . . . danceable. And I had an immediate image in my mind: me and Jesus, waltzing around the Communion Table. God, I loved that moment so much. I cherished it as a weird, delightful spiritual experience long before I could acknowledge with confidence what I now believe: that image was a gift from God. A consolation. No wonder nearly thirty years later I'll be getting a doctor of ministry in imagination. That's how God has always managed to capture my attention.

One last thing, because I love a holy coincidence. The requiem ended with "eternal light" rendered in Latin: *et lux perpetua*. You can imagine my thrill when the liturgy at Covenant echoed the same phrase: "We rest in your eternal light." How about that.

In the love and eternal light of Christ,
Katherine

March 24, 2023

Dear Katherine,

I've written three letters that I haven't sent, but this, the fourth, will make its way to you. I was so happy to have you at my baptism, although in a different context than originally planned. It was the right thing, to be baptized at my church, by my pastor, but I understand your twinge of grief and I don't fault you for it. Neither do I fault you for your discomfort in being a female pastor in a Presbyterian Church in America congregation, which bars the ordination of women. I've been toiling away on another letter about this, but for now I'll just say that many, many people in that sanctuary believe what you and I do: God always intended for women to preach, eventually. I'll leave it at that for now.

Baptism is funny. I know I don't get to define the meaning of a sacrament, but I'm going to anyway (isn't my relationship with God as valid as anything?), and we're both just going to have to live with my theology's divergence from doctrine. Anyway. I don't believe that my baptism saved me; Jesus redeemed me before I was so much as an idea in my mother's head. What I do believe, and what causes me a great deal of anxiety, is that baptism formalizes my relationship with God and the church. It signifies a covenant agreement that I will look to God, recognize my need for him, and seek to live a life like Christ. This is of course impossible to carry off flawlessly. I'm not so self-aggrandizing to imagine that I singularly struggle with sin, but I am a perfectionist who cannot abide by my own failings. They hound me and they haunt me. I am likewise haunted by my vulnerability to a particular category of sin, and if we are to take Paul's warnings at face value, I am on the road to perdition. It's so common as to be boring, were the cost not so high, but no one around me understands it, let alone struggles similarly. I feel that I am the worst of my friends. The weakest, and willful as they come.

I can't remember which theologian spoke of this so poignantly, maybe Kierkegaard, but the attitude towards sin matters. It's one thing to stumble into it, and another to look it square in the face, call it by name, and invite it into the interior castle (Teresa of Avila). I am not so foolish with envy, greed, or pride. I am not powerless in the face of every sin, but where I am weak I am damn near worthless. A little idol factory, worshiping at the shrines of lust and betrayal. It's not pleasure that I seek at the heart of it, though; it's anesthesia. It all begins with pain, intolerable pain, and the joke is that as numb as I make myself, it also ends with pain. "I am a house gutted by fire where only the guilty sometimes sleep before the punishment that devours them hounds them out into the open."[2] I am the house as much as I am the guilty, harassed and homeless. Completely aware, completely ablaze.

I met with a spiritual director from my church right before I sat down to write this letter, and despite my best efforts to convince her otherwise, she would not agree that I am hell bound. I think I will keep inquiring with higher spiritual minds until someone at last confirms that God will forsake me, because I do not know how to reconcile infinite love with infallible justice. I'm not afraid of the judgment, so long as it's a purging of imperfection and not banishment, but what if it's the latter? Beth, the spiritual director, thinks that as long as I keep saying yes to God, that I will find my way out of this vicious cycle. She, like Teresa of Avila, seems to believe that "God will draw out the good even from [my] fall," and that resonates. Maybe, like St. Teresa says, "Sometimes it is actually God's will that we are plagued by bad thoughts we cannot get rid of and spiritual aridity we cannot alleviate."[3] I love this, and it shouldn't surprise me as much as it does. Why wouldn't even my transgressions factor into God's plan? Am I so faithless to suggest that God didn't foresee, and maybe plan for, all of this? I'm changing my mind as I'm writing. Maybe I am stuck because God wants me stuck. Maybe I am not ready to be anywhere else. Granted, I'm due for some unpleasant natural consequences, but from God I can accept them. Suffering feels different when earned, different when it comes from love.

Beth said I shouldn't hate myself, and I agree. I know God doesn't want that for me or anyone. He wants us to forgive ourselves as he forgives us, and to keep turning for as long as it takes to start walking in the right direction. I want to forgive myself, but my defiance tortures me. St. Teresa, who reportedly missed the same marks I do, says, "This voice of his is so sweet that the poor soul falls apart in the face of her own inability to instantly do whatever he asks of her,"[4] and I have nothing to amend or add. It is this. The pain is precisely this.

Today I am coming out of the fog in which I've been lost for weeks.
Love,
Devon

2. Rilke, *Book of Hours*, 137.
3. Teresa of Avila, *Interior Castle*, 61.
4. Teresa of Avila, *Interior Castle*, 56.

March 31, 2023

Dear Katherine,

Last night, I was at a church for your event, and someone asked me about my baptism. You must have told him something about it, because I only mentioned it in passing, and the first thing he expressed was surprise that I belong to the Presbyterian Church in America. He asked if I chose it based on the theology or the people. Though the answer is both, I wouldn't be at Covenant if not for the orthodoxy and liturgy, and I told him so. I've never spoken of my theology to that group of people, so he must have made an assumption.

I felt exposed, like someone had torn off a disguise to reveal that I am no uber-liberal, mainline Christian, and had been passing all along. He aired his grievance that First Congo seemed to shy away from defining most of their beliefs, perhaps for fear of alienating anyone, and I said something about Christianity having fundamental tenets and those not being up for debate. At this point, a woman nearby offered the defense that congregants at her church *are* unified in their belief in Christ, and because I thought I knew where she was going (assumptions, assumptions), I chimed in with, "Right, that he was the son of God, sent out of love for us to die for our sins, and resurrected." What she went on to say was that Christ "actually existed and was a real historical figure that walked the earth." I was appalled. We can edit the edges out of that adjective later, but if I'm honest, it's how I felt. I was horrified, but also filled with a slimy, pharisaical judgment. I absolutely judged her for what I deemed an insipid and erroneous view of Christ. I flagellated myself on the drive home, cognizant of the sin in my heart, if not on my lips, ruminating on my failure to love.

Here, I need to make a slight detour in the narrative. In February, I purchased an illuminated gospel by Makoto Fujimura as a birthday gift for Ian. He had told me about the book and I knew he would love it. I wanted to give him something beautiful, but he has since all but disappeared from my life (For weeks this time? Months? Forever?), so I never celebrated his birthday with him. Out of more faith than that relationship deserves, I kept the book in my possession for our next meeting. The days crept into weeks, then a month, then more, and the relationship unraveled in its typical fashion, without conversation or conflict, but still some naive part of me imagined that he wouldn't do this to me again, that this time he would keep his promise and stay put, and that the book would be waiting for him when he proved my fears of abandonment wrong. In the past week I have felt very close to God, and on the guidance of the incredible spiritual director I met with last week, I have been trying to know God's will through the doors he opens. The door that is this particular relationship has slammed shut on me so many times, crushing fingers and toes too stubborn to get out of the way, and each time I have remained on the other side of that door, banging until it reopens. In the past week, as I've lingered on the threshold of that pitiless door, I couldn't help but notice the obvious: it was closed, and I'm not so sure anymore that God wants me to beat my fists bloody trying to get back through. It's not like the Gospel of Luke's parable of the friend at midnight, because the man on the other side of this door is not God, and what's waiting for me is not the kingdom of heaven. I'm starting to think that maybe God himself closed that door.

Back to my failure to love. When I arrived home last night, weary from regret, something moved me to take the gift out of its hermetically sealed wrapping and read the book. I leafed through the first pages before opening it to a black ribbon that marked Matthew 23, and Jesus's seven woes to the scribes and Pharisees, which could have been addressed directly to me. As Jesus convicted them, he condemned my own hypocrisy and the judgment in my heart for the woman. Who am I, willful and vain and materialistic, to judge another's faith? "Right" or "wrong" theology has nothing to do with it (and I still think I'm right, by the way)—it's simply not my place. That woman has her relationship with Jesus and I have mine, and if God has any issues with either, he'll deal with them himself. In Jesus's warnings to the Pharisees, I came to know myself, but I did not feel shamed. What I experienced instead was the grace inherent in guidance, and a chance to change. I asked for forgiveness and forgave myself, pledging repentance, and in return I received peace. I wish the climax of this story had occurred somewhere less banal, but it happened while brushing my teeth that night. I'm not sure if it was myself or God, but a voice cut through the rumbling of my electric toothbrush and said, "The gospel is yours."

I decided to keep that book.

Love,
Devon

April 12, 2023

Dear Devon,

 Christ is Risen! I am all in on the season of Easter this year. I need Eastertide, fifty whole days to contemplate and celebrate the Resurrection. You said that you've been feeling close to God lately and I hope this continues to be true for you. It is true for me, too. It was a gift to preach on Easter Sunday, and to respond again to the Spirit's invitation to memorize the text. I can't tell you how much I loved circling my neighborhood before dawn on Easter Sunday, reciting the Scripture again and again. My friends who do this regularly call it "interiorizing" the text, and I think this is a better description than mere memorization. The Word goes deeper than just the mind and memory; you truly do learn it by heart. I know that you're working on memorizing Colossians and I am tempted to join you in that endeavor. ("Tempted" is probably the wrong word. But perhaps we can be tempted by goodness as readily as we can be tempted by sin.)

 I have to admit that in addition to the full days of Holy Week keeping me from writing back, I've also struggled to know how best to respond to your interaction with the band members about theology. (I am sorry I "outed" you—I did not know you weren't "out," and I hope it doesn't become an obstacle in your relationships with members here.) I don't want to be defensive about the theological liberalism of my tradition, nor do I want to debate doctrine. And yet, my first reaction was indeed defensive and disputative—but not perhaps in the way you'd think. One of the things I genuinely love about the United Church of Christ is that it creates space for all different types of Christians. High Christology and low Christology are both respected and validated. I don't think our lack of clear and unified doctrine is a failure; to me, it reflects an intrinsic humility and a radical hospitality. Our unity rests not on fundamentals but on the Spirit's movement to gather us as a congregation. It's not that I don't care what my parishioners believe. But I have my convictions, and as one of the people entrusted to inhabit the pulpit, I get to preach and teach about Jesus as I understand him, and hopefully nurture the faith of the whole spectrum of believers in this place.

 Here's where it gets tricky: I think the statements you and the woman at my church swapped are right, yet in their own way, incomplete. To be fair, you were both aiming to name what you believed to be *fundamental* about

Jesus, not comprehensive. She offered up the fact that Jesus "actually existed and was a real historical figure that walked the earth." There is no lie here. He did actually exist, and he was a real historical figure that walked the earth. His life mattered. Now, I have a lot to say about why his life mattered. I believe he is the Son of God and wholeheartedly confess that to behold Jesus is to behold God. I believe that his preaching, teaching, and healing revealed the breadth and depth of God's already-but-not-yet Kingdom. I believe that his love and life were so perfect, so utterly full of goodness, that a broken and sinful humanity could not tolerate it, and tried to stifle it. Did, in fact. I believe that our real historical figure suffered and died on the cross, and that in an act of profound love and mercy, God raised him on the third day. I believe the Risen Christ walked the earth again, encountering many of the same people who had been his disciples. I believe he ascended to heaven and sent the Holy Spirit to dwell among us, empowering us to be the church. And I believe that absolutely nothing will ever be the same because of the life, death, and resurrection of Jesus Christ. (My heart rate quickened as I typed that paragraph. Happy Easter! Christ is Risen!)

Now, much of what I said in that last paragraph is more or less compatible with your statement, that Jesus was "the son of God, sent out of love for us to die for our sins, and resurrected." Or maybe it's not. Maybe that paragraph reads like so much liberal Christianity-lite to you. But we certainly agree that Jesus was the Son of God, and that he was resurrected. I also am 100 percent on board that Jesus was sent out of love for us. But I hesitate to affirm that Jesus was sent to *die*—or at least, I hesitate to affirm it without affirming that he was equally sent to *live*. When asked if Jesus was born to die, the late Rachel Held Evans countered, "A lot of times people talk about Jesus as though God is mad at mankind so God sends Jesus to save us from ourselves, so the whole point was for Jesus to come and to die and to save us from our sins so we could go to heaven. A lot of times this leaves the whole story and Jesus's teachings completely out of the Christian faith as though they're kind of inconsequential, like back story to the cross. But Jesus's teachings matter." In the same interview, she said this: "I look at Jesus and I see God dying before holding our sins against us. I see God choosing to hang on the cross and choosing to forgive rather than hold our sins against us."[1] Maybe this is just another way of saying that Jesus was sent to die, but I'm not sure.

---

1. Evans, "Risking It on Jesus."

I find myself wanting to stand in the vast crevasse between those two statements, and say, "Yes, and . . . " to both of them.

Even after writing all this out, I worry I missed the point of your letter—after all, it didn't end with you fuming about "insipid and erroneous" beliefs about Jesus. It ended with you experiencing gospel grace and peace. It's entirely possible that I am still responding in defensiveness, and if that is the case, I am once again sorry. (I apologize a lot these days.) I guess I do feel a certain protectiveness about my congregation and parishioners. They are my flock. I totally get it that the Reformed and Presbyterian Church in America traditions put a high value on doctrine, and that in comparison the United Church of Christ tradition can seem theologically flimsy. But at the end of the day—perhaps when we're brushing our teeth—I trust that the Holy Spirit is at work in all of us, coaxing all of us into gospel grace and peace.

I love you, and I hope that you're still feeling filled by your baptism and the glory of Easter.

Love,
Katherine

April 15, 2023

Dear Katherine,

I just listened to your sermon from a few weeks ago, and I wept. It wasn't because your message was sad—it was the opposite—but I grieve for your grief. I am so sad about your sadness. I am also astonished at your ability to use your pain to worship Christ, as I so often fail to do. I have a different kind of sadness about your response to my letter. It almost seems like you stopped reading after the first two paragraphs—not even to the last line of the second—and missed the entire point of what I tried to express. You wrote, "One of the things I genuinely love about the United Church of Christ is that it creates space for all different types of Christians." I wrote, "Who am I, willful and vain and materialistic, to judge another's faith? 'Right' or 'wrong' theology has nothing to do with it." These statements align. I expected that using an anecdote about your church would elicit some personal feelings, but I also hoped you would be able to see and accept my humility. It's a gamble, writing about the ugliness inside of me, because every confession risks judgment and misunderstanding. I don't feel judged, but I feel misunderstood. I was trying to write about learning to be better.

It's my fault for not writing with more precision, so here I need to clarify that I do not think Christ was sent *only* to die, but was very much also sent to live. Henri Nouwen, Donald McNeil, and Douglas Morrison sum up the selling point (for me) of Christianity: "The mystery of God's love is not that he takes our pain away, but that he first wants to share them with us."[1] God, the inventor of empathy, chose to feel how we feel. He also chose to defeat death for our sake, which involved dying. The authors above remind us that crucifixion is "a death that we 'normal' humans would hardly be willing to consider ours,"[2] which to me suggests that Jesus was and is *even more human* than the rest of us. Of course Jesus came to live. His teachings on earth are the literal gospel. But he also died, on purpose, for us. Without death there is no resurrection. Without resurrection, in *my* theology, there is no Christianity.

---

1. Nouwen et al., *Compassion*, 18.
2. Nouwen et al., *Compassion*, 26.

I intended to write a letter about purity culture and hedonism, but I have yoga and a voice lesson to get to.

To be continued.

Love,
Devon

April 15, 2023

Dear Devon,

    First, thank you for your kind words and sympathetic tears about the sermon. I am wildly grateful that I was assigned to preach on a Lenten Sunday before I was responsible for preaching the Easter message. I desperately needed to speak about grief, because it was all I could think about, and the story of Lazarus was the perfect text for my context. Last Sunday I leaned as far into the joy of Easter as I possibly could. Not that the grief still isn't acute; Easter just wasn't the day to bring it into the pulpit with me.

    I am sorry my response saddened you, and made you feel misunderstood. I think I did understand—at least mostly—what you were communicating. The anecdote about my church just felt so personal to me. I was not mature enough to have just let it be the background for the *real* story, even though the real story was a moving and beautiful one. To hear you describe that you were horrified by one of my parishioner's "insipid and erroneous" beliefs stung, and turned me into a bit of a mama bear. And so instead of dwelling on the unexpected twist, I inserted myself into the scene and defended what did not need defending.

    I am off to a reunion for the Guatemala trip—more soon, but I love you, and I trust that we will continue to give one another grace.

Love,
Katherine

April 24, 2023

Dear Devon,

 It is almost the second day of May. That day will mark three months since my father's death. And it will mark one full year of exchanging these love letters to God. And while I'm musing about death, it was just fifteen days into this project that my father-in-law succumbed to Parkinson's disease. What a year. I'm grateful to have these letters as a record of my days—not just of the big stuff, but the ordinary moments that made it onto these pages. I'm grateful for the record of *your* days, as well. It's been quite a year for you, too. It has been such a profound honor to receive your letters. I can't imagine we'll ever be done with this blessed genre. Ours will be a friendship that integrates the written word and the coffee date.

 I am writing this letter today because I want it on the permanent record that this morning's coffee date was precious. Sacred. I told you I woke up this morning in a happy-go-lucky mood. I listened to Paul Zach's new song, "Beautiful World," on repeat. I squealed with delight over the presence of the swings for grown-ups at the coffee shop. (Swings! In a coffee shop!) And then somehow I ended up needing a whole stack of napkins with which to wipe my eyes and blow my nose. But I was in good company; you needed a few, too. I am so grateful we revisited some tender spots in our friendship with such vulnerability and empathy. We both know it could have gone the other way. We could have raised our hackles. We could have shuttered our hearts. But we didn't. We held hands over that gorgeous burrito you were eating and we chose to trust that the Holy Spirit is actively working within and among us. We chose to find our unity in Christ. We chose to love one another, because love is from God.

 What a gift.

 I love you.

Peace,
Katherine

Afterword

THIS BOOK HAS NO ENDING. Much like life, which Christians know as eternal, this book continues beyond its final page, because the book *is* our relationship, and creation is as inherently relational as the triune God, the ultimate artist. The Father, Son, and Holy spirit exist in a never-ending feedback loop of love, trust, and service, and I have come to think of this book in similar terms. The union between Katherine, myself, and God inspired and propelled the project, and the three of us cycle on to this day. For this reason, I will not answer the question of "where are they now," at least not with specificity. What I will tell you is that much has changed. Neither of us lives where we lived, I do not love whom I loved, and even our friendship looks different than before. Certainly my theology continues to evolve. It would make for a tidier arc if these letters built to a climax and collapsed into resolution, but it would not be real. Life has no end, and neither does this book.

What then is the point of a book without a thesis? Katherine invited me into this exchange as a dissertation stand-in for her doctor of ministry, and in the same breath suggested we turn it into a book. A real book. A book published by a real company and marketed to real readers. A book I never expected would see the light of day. I had never published anything and had no reason to expect that would change. I didn't see the promise Katherine did and couldn't fathom why anyone would care about my ideas, which made it much easier to say yes. I could think and write with abandon, knowing my words would reach only Katherine and her program head, who himself would care only about his pupil's work. I didn't plan my letters, didn't edit them, didn't read them. I wrote without direction or intention. I wrote to write. Most of us gravitate toward teleologic activity, pursuing one thing or another in order to reach a goal, but I wrote for the sake of it. I wrote because with every thought expressed, I moved closer to my friend and my faith. I wrote myself toward God. If I had written with

Afterword

a destination in mind I would never have arrived there, because this book is a seventy-thousand-word prayer. This book did not, could not, have a thesis, because this book is a love letter to God. Never-ending as prayer; never-ending as life.

The question remains: *What is the point of a book without a thesis?* The point of this book is the point of prayer. For a moment, put aside your faith and lean into the most scientific part of you—the part that needs "proof." What the world considers "reason" looks askance at prayer, and rightly so. How many prayers has God met with seeming silence? Jesus himself could not get an answer when he agonized in the garden, and if the Father saw fit to respond to the Son with silence, we must resign ourselves to the same. It's true that God sometimes delivers our desires on a silver platter, but we cannot know what God feels and thinks when we beseech him, and more often than not we read between the lines of life to glean an answer that may or may not be there. To the rational mind, prayer is nothing more than a nice idea. But what is prayer to the penitent? What is prayer to the Christian, who feels God's presence as visceral as an embrace when she cries out to him? What is prayer to the agnostic, who begs a God he's never encountered to safely land his plane? What is prayer to the atheist, who prays for God to save a life she isn't convinced God ever created? Prayer is everything. Sometimes, it is literally everything. Screaming to the silent heavens, praying the rosary, or falling on one's knees in adoration gives us something ineffable. Something happens when I recite the Lord's Prayer, silently, in my head, thrice daily. I have grown more through prayer, and the answers I get, than through my fancy degrees and overpriced postgraduate certifications. I have known myself more through prayer than through any helpful but overwhelmingly limited sessions with a therapist. It was prayer that put an end to my chronic infidelities. Prayer that stopped my destruction in its tracks. Prayer is *everything*, and these letters are prayers. The point is prayer.

I do not know how you, our reader, felt as we wailed, cajoled, and worshiped God through these letters. Did they even feel like praying to you? Did you relate to our anxieties, or did we alienate you? When Wipf & Stock offered to publish this book, their letter sat unanswered in my inbox for weeks, a casualty of anxiety. I was paralyzed by the fear that readers would judge my developing theology, writing, or worse yet, my intellect (i.e., ego). I steeled myself for bad reviews and nasty comments, and comforted myself with the possibility that no one but my mother would actually read what I

Afterword

had written. Many times I wanted to relegate the project to obscurity, but for months I begged God for a reason to keep it all hidden and did not receive the answer I wanted. I still feel uneasy about making my thoughts public, but I can't control your experience and I don't want to. I'll never know what compelled you to read a book of letters between two women you've never heard of, but since you did, I hope you felt a glimmer of what Katherine and I did when we wrote it.

If I had my way, you would walk away with the freedom to explore. I have the double good fortune of coming to faith as an adult and landing in an intellectually bent church, and I am too old and too self-possessed to let anyone shut down my questioning. Shamefully for the church, that is not a prototypical experience. Jesus spoke in parables, so I'm going to go out on a limb and suggest he was a proponent of critical thinking, but not all traditions follow this biblical one. Far too many churches rely on fear instead of faith in the gospel to keep people close, and if the staggering number of Christians abandoning their faith is any indication, it's not a good strategy. If you made it to the end of this book, you had a front-row seat to my fumbling, grasping, and periodically straight-up inaccurate interpretations of Scripture, and a part of me hates that exposure. Another part of me, a better part of me, hopes that witnessing it gave you license to do the same. You should read the Bible, cover to cover, and you should ask and challenge and search. You should feel uncomfortable when Scripture is uncomfortable, and sit in it long enough to find God in the mess of it. You should throw out my imperatives and explore whatever and however you want after you put down this book. I needed, still need, to let my thoughts run wild before they find their resting place, and I want the same for you. God wants you to engage with him. Do it.

My second wish is to impart the Christian dichotomy of freedom: you may stay bound. In this increasingly secular age of replacing faith with irreligious ideologies, Christianity does not always fare well. We are right to hold the church responsible for crimes perpetrated against humanity, and Christians accountable for their sins, but we must stop short of vilification. For all our base humanity and the problems it causes, Christians are not terrible, unforgivable humans down to the last. More importantly, though ours is a beautiful, life-changing, life-saving, community-building, grace-bestowing, justice-seeking faith, the secular world at worst reduces us down to our errors and at best misunderstands. We do not acknowledge the sinful nature at our core to shame, but to comfort and liberate from expectations we will surely fail to meet. We follow commandments not out of arbitrary rigidity, but to avoid hurting others and ourselves. If anyone reads the Bible and a history of the ancient Near East at the same time, they will learn that Christian tenets protected women, children, widows, and orphans, and I beg them to consider that context today. I want you, our reader, to know that it is okay to claim your Christianity. There is nothing wrong with having faith—everything is right about your love of God—no matter what anyone says, no matter what you read. If you have been insulted, mischaracterized, shamed, or frightened, know that we have you. We all have you. You are an invaluable member of the body of Christ, and we cherish you. I don't know your gender, race, nationality, political affiliation, height, or favorite color, but I know your faith, and it is beautiful. Nothing could be more beautiful.

Finally, I hope this book moves you to seek what Katherine and I built: a relationship with Christ between you. Kierkegaard said it (and everything) better than anyone when he wrote, "To help another human being to love God is to love another man; to be helped by another human being to love God is to be loved."[1] I am not so exclusive or close-minded to circle the wagons around myself and my church community, leaving my family, clients, and any number of other loved ones to fend for themselves on the perimeter, but I long for the explicit presence of Jesus in all of my relationships. God is present when my brother and I put aside our tumultuous past to connect as adults, and in my dear friend's unshakable support, but with them he goes about in disguise. With Katherine, as with all my Christian loved ones, God stands before and between us, resplendent in unnakedobscured glory. He is not only named, but the protagonist of every story. He is the locus of connection, and the individual bonds we share with him invite us into a more vivid intimacy with one another. The manifestation of God between two people is the genesis of love and a microcosm of creation. When God appears before two people, their eyes wide in recognition, it is as if he said to the relationship, "Let there be light." And all of a sudden, through this small miracle, it comes to life.

Devon Spencer

---

1. Kierkegaard, *Works of Love*, 112.

Bibliography

Augustine, Saint. *Confessions.* Translated by Garry Wills. Penguin Classics. London: Penguin, 2008.

Barnes, M. Craig. "Pastor, Not Friend." *Christian Century* 130 (Jan. 9, 2013) 27–28.

Bauerschmidt, Frederick Christian. *The Love That Is God: An Invitation to Christian Faith.* Grand Rapids: Eerdmans, 2020.

Borg, Marcus. *Convictions: How I Learned What Matters Most.* San Francisco: Harper Collins, 2014.

Buechner, Frederick. *Wishful Thinking.* San Francisco: HarperCollins, 1973.

Detweiler, Linford, and Karin Bergquist. "All My Favorite People." Track 12 on *The Long Surrender.* Produced by Joe Henry. Cincinnati: Great Speckled Dog, 2011.

Ellul, Jacques. *Violence: Reflections from a Christian Perspective.* Jacques Ellul Legacy. Eugene, OR: Wipf & Stock, 2012.

Evans, Rachel Held. "Risking It on Jesus." The Work of the People, n.d. https://www.theworkofthepeople.com/risking-it-on-jesus.

Fawcett, John. "Blest Be the Tie That Binds." Hymnary, 1782. https://hymnary.org/text/blest_be_the_tie_that_binds.

Gilbert, Jack. "A Brief for the Defense." *Sun,* July 2013.

Goodall, Howard. "In Paradisum—Lux Aeterna." Track 10 of *Eternal Light: A Requiem.* 2008. http://www.howardgoodall.co.uk/works/choral-music/eternal-light/eternal-light-full-text.

Heschel, Abraham J. *The Prophets.* New York: HarperCollins, 2023.

Hesla, Bret. *Dazzling Bouquet.* Minneapolis: Fortress, 1995.

Ignatieff, Michael. "The Art of Consolation." Persuasion, Nov. 23, 2022. https://open.substack.com/pub/persuasion1/p/the-art-of-consolation?utm_source=direct&utm_campaign=post&utm_medium=web.

Jaouad, Suleika. *Between Two Kingdoms: A Memoir of a Life Interrupted.* New York: Random House, 2021.

Johnson, Trygve. "Introduction: Eugene H. Peterson Center for Christian Imagination." Address given at Doxology conference, Holland, MI, October 17, 2022.

Jones, Beth Felker. "Embodied from Creation Through Redemption: Placing Gender and Sexuality in Theological Context." In *Beauty, Order, and Mystery: A Christian Vision of Human Sexuality,* edited by Gerald L. Hiestand and Todd Wilson, 21–30. Center for Pastor Theologians. Lisle, IL: InterVarsity, 2017.

Kierkegaard, Søren. *The Essential Kierkegaard.* Translated by Howard V. Hong and Edna H. Hong. Princeton, NJ: Princeton University Press, 2023.

———. *Fear and Trembling.* London: Merchant, 2012.

BIBLIOGRAPHY

———. *Works of Love*. Translated by Howard Hong and Edna Hong. Harper Perennial Modern Thought. San Francisco: HarperCollins, 1962.
Lawrence, Brother. *"The Practice of the Presence of God" and "The Spiritual Maxims."* UK: Dover, 2023.
Lewis, C. S. *The Screwtape Letters*. New York: Macmillan, 1966.
Luther, Martin. "Preface to the Revelation of St. John (1522)." University Lutheran Church, n.d. From *Word and Sacrament I*, edited by E. Theodore Bachmann, 398–99, vol. 35 of *Luther's Works* (Philadelphia: Fortress, 1960). https://www.universitylutheran.church/luther-on-revelation.html.
MacDonald, George. *Unspoken Sermons*. London: Longmans, Green & Co., 1906.
Mackie, Tim, et al., hosts. BibleProject, Dec. 6, 2021. *The Paradigm*, episode 12, "How (Not) to Read the Bible." https://bibleproject.com/podcast/how-not-read-bible/.
McKelvey, Douglas. "A Liturgy for Missing Someone." In *Every Moment Holy*, vol. 2. IOS or Android, Brentwood, 2021.
Michel, Jen Pollock. *Teach Us to Want: Longing, Ambition, and the Life of Faith*. Lisle, IL: IVP, 2014.
Nouwen, Henri J. M. *The Inner Voice of Love*. New York: Random House, 1998.
———. *Letters to Marc About Jesus*. San Francisco: HarperCollins, 2007. Ebook.
———. *With Open Hands*. Notre Dame, IN: Ave Maria, 2006.
Nouwen, Henri J. M., et al. *Compassion: A Reflection on the Christian Life*. New York: Doubleday, 1983.
Peterson, Eugene. "Answering God." *On Being*, Dec. 22, 2016; last updated Apr. 7, 2022. With Krista Tippett. https://onbeing.org/programs/eugene-peterson-answering-god/.
Peterson, Eugene H. *Answering God: The Psalms as Tools for Prayer*. San Francisco: HarperOne, 1991.
———. *On Living Well*. Colorado Springs: Waterbrook, 2021.
———. *Reversed Thunder: The Revelation of John and the Praying Imagination*. San Francisco: HarperOne, 1988.
———. *Run with the Horses: The Quest for Life at Its Best*. Lisle, IL: IVP, 2022.
———. *Where Your Treasure Is: Psalms That Summon You from Self to Community*. Grand Rapids: Eerdmans, 1993.
Rilke, Rainer Maria. *Rilke's Book of Hours: Love Poems to God*. Translated by Anita Barrows and Joanna Macy. New York: Penguin, 2005.
Robinson, Marilynne. *Gilead*. New York: Picador, 2004.
Root, Andrew. *Faith Formation in a Secular Age*. Ada, MI: Baker Academic, 2017.
Rose, Matthew. "Tayloring Christianity." *First Things*, Dec. 1, 2014. https://www.firstthings.com/article/2014/12/tayloring-christianity.
Saxe, John Godfrey. "The Blind Men and the Elephant." CommonLit, 1873. https://www.commonlit.org/texts/the-blind-men-and-the-elephant.
Scott, Sophfronia. *Love's Long Line*. Columbus, OH: Mad Creek, 2018.
Shakespeare, William. *Macbeth*. London: Dicks, 1871.
Teresa of Avila. *The Interior Castle*. Translated by Mirabai Starr. London: Penguin, 2004.
Wiman, Christian. *My Bright Abyss*. New York: Farrar, Straus and Giroux, 2013.